*This book is dedicated to the memory of my
two grandmothers, Margaret Trott and Simone McCauley,
each of whom treasured books and whose love of reading
informs all of my work.*

Read On . . . Crime Fiction

Reading Lists for Every Taste

Barry Trott

Read On Series

A Member of the Greenwood Publishing Group

Westport, Connecticut • London

Library of Congress Cataloging-in-Publication Data

Trott, Barry, 1961–
   Read on—crime fiction : reading lists for every taste / Barry Trott.
      p. cm.—(Read on series)
   Includes index.
   ISBN 978–1–59158–373–8 (alk. paper)
   1. Detective and mystery stories, American—Bibliography. 2. Detective and mystery stories, English—Bibliography. 3. Crime—Fiction—Bibliography. I. Title.
   Z1231.D47T76   2008
   [PS374.D4]
   016.823'087208—dc22   2007033858

British Library Cataloguing in Publication Data is available.

Library of Congress Catalog Card Number: 2007033858
ISBN: 978–1–59158–373–8

First published in 2008

Libraries Unlimited, 88 Post Road West, Westport, CT 06881
A Member of the Greenwood Publishing Group, Inc.
www.lu.com

Printed in the United States of America

The paper used in this book complies with the
Permanent Paper Standard issued by the National
Information Standards Organization (Z39.48–1984).

10 9 8 7 6 5 4 3 2 1

Contents

Series Foreword

Welcome to Libraries Unlimited's Read On series of genre guides for readers' advisors and for readers. The Read On series introduces readers and those who work with them to new ways of looking at books, genres, and reading interests.

Over the past decade, readers' advisory services have become vital in public libraries. A quick glance at the schedule of any library conference at the state or national level will reveal a wealth of programs on various aspects of connecting readers to books they will enjoy. Working with unfamiliar genres or types of reading can be a challenge, particularly for those new to the field. Equally, readers may find it a bit overwhelming to look for books outside their favorite authors and preferred reading interests. The titles in the Read On series offer you a new way to approach reading:

- they introduce you to a broad sampling of the materials available in a given genre;
- they offer you new directions to explore in a genre—through appeal features and unconventional topics;
- they help readers' advisors better understand and navigate genres with which they are less familiar;
- and they provide reading lists that you can use to create quick displays, include on your library web sites and in the library newsletter, or to hand out to readers.

The lists in the Read On series are arranged in sections based on appeal characteristics—story, character, setting, and language (as described in Joyce Saricks' Reader's Advisory Services in the Public Library, 3d ed., ALA Editions, 2005), with a fifth section on mood. These appeal characteristics are the hidden elements of a book that attract readers. Remember that a book can have multiple appeal factors; and sometimes readers are drawn to a particular book for several factors, while other times for only one. In the Read On lists, titles are placed according to their primary appeal characteristics, and then put into a list that reflects common reading interests. So if you are working with a reader who loves fantasy that features quests for magical objects you will be able to find a list of titles whose main appeal centers around this search. Each list indicates a title that is an especially good starting place for readers, an exemplar of that appeal characteristic.

Story is perhaps the most basic appeal characteristic. It relates to the plot of the book—what are the elements of the tale? Is the emphasis more on the people or the situations? Is the story action focused or more interior? Is it funny? Scary?

Many readers are drawn to the books they love by the characters. The character appeal reflects such aspects as whether there are lots of characters or only a single main character; are the characters easily recognizable types? Do the characters grow and change over the course of the story? What are the characters' occupations?

Setting covers a range of elements that might appeal to readers. What is the time period or geographic locale of the tale? How much does the author describe the surroundings of the story? Does the reader feel as though he or she is "there" when reading the book? Are there special features such as the monastic location of Ellis Peters' Brother Cadfael mysteries or the small town setting of Jan Karon's Mitford series?

Although not traditionally considered an appeal characteristic, mood is important to readers as well. It relates to how the author uses the tools of narrative—language, pacing, story, and character—to create a feeling for the work. Mood can be difficult to quantify because the reader brings his or her own feelings to the story as well. Mood really asks how does the book make the reader feel? Creepy? Refreshed? Joyful? Sad?

Finally, the language appeal brings together titles where the author's writing style draws the reader. This can be anything from a lyrical prose style with lots of flourishes to a spare use of language à la Hemingway. Humor, snappy dialog, wordplay, recipes and other language elements all have the potential to attract readers.

Dig into these lists. Use them to find new titles and authors in a genre that you love, or as a guide to expand your knowledge of a new type of writing. Above all, read, enjoy, and remember—never apologize for your reading tastes!

Barry Trott
Series Editor

Acknowledgments

I would like to thank all of my colleagues at the Williamsburg Regional Library for their support and their enthusiasm for reading and talking about books. Also, thanks to all the readers' advisors with whom I have had the pleasure of talking about mysteries over the past several years. Thanks especially to editor extraordinaire Barbara Ittner for her help in shaping this book and the entire Read On series. And finally, special thanks to Lynn and Eleanor Trott for their gift of time to work on this book and for their thoughts and comments about crime fiction and the lists in the book.

Introduction

Crime Fiction Defined

Crime fiction is enjoyed by a wide range of readers, and each one would have his or her own definition of what makes for a good crime story. For some readers, the details of the investigation are a primary interest, for others, it might be the setting or the time period, whereas other readers enjoy puzzling out the solution along with the detective. There are readers who want to know all the gory details of the crime, while others want all the death to occur offstage.

Despite the variety of appeals, there are some basic elements that all the titles listed in the following lists share. At the foundation, mystery stories involve a crime being committed, the investigation into that crime, and some resolution to the investigation. Within these relatively straightforward parameters, the writer of crime fiction can take myriad paths. The killer can be divulged early on in the story, increasing the suspense as the paths of the murderer and the detective draw closer. Conversely, the solution to the crime can remain a puzzle up to the last page. The author may be liberal or stingy with clues to the identity of the criminal. Early works of crime fiction generally saw the criminal brought to some formal justice, giving a clear end to the story, but some contemporary crime fiction takes a grayer view of the meting out of justice. Criminals sometimes get away or are beyond the reach of the law.

The titles listed give a sampling of the broad appeal of contemporary crime fiction. Readers looking for a cozy story for a cold winter night will find as much to enjoy here as readers looking for gritty, hard-boiled detectives. So read on and dig into a great mystery.

A Brief History of Crime Fiction

Crime fiction can be said to start with Genesis, chapter four, verses 1 to 16. Cain resents Abel, lures him out into the fields, and kills him. After a brief interrogation in which he denies any knowledge, Cain confesses, and he is punished. That is crime fiction at its most elemental. There are other stories of crime and punishment throughout the next couple of millennia, but it is not until the 1840s that crime fiction really becomes its own genre. In that decade, Edgar

Allan Poe published three stories featuring an amateur detective who is able to solve crimes that have baffled the police. "The Murders in the Rue Morgue," published in 1841, introduced readers to Auguste Dupin, who solves crimes by thought rather than action.

In the late nineteenth century, the next great leap in crime fiction occurred when Arthur Conan Doyle introduced that paragon of ratiocination, Sherlock Holmes, beginning with "A Study in Scarlet" (1887). Holmes became the model for legions of future investigators, with his eccentric habits, keen powers of observation, sometimes superhuman abilities, and, of course, his faithful sidekick, Dr. Watson. This duo continued to solve crimes for the next 40 years, finally closing their partnership in *The Case-Book of Sherlock Holmes* (1927).

The success of Holmes encouraged other crime-fiction writers on both sides of the Atlantic, and the decades beginning just prior to World War I and proceeding up to World War II are often known as the golden age of crime fiction. The golden age saw the flourishing of the puzzle-based crime story. During this time, G .K Chesterton introduced his priestly sleuth, Father Brown (*The Innocence of Father Brown,* 1911). Of course, the queen of the golden age was Agatha Christie, whose two detective series, featuring Miss Marple (*The Murder at the Vicarage,* 1930) and Hercule Poirot (*The Mysterious Affair at Styles,* 1920), are much imitated. The golden age also featured notable writers such as Dorothy Sayers, who introduced aristocratic sleuth Lord Peter Wimsey in *Whose Body?* (1923), and Ellery Queen (*The Roman Hat Mystery,* 1929). The golden age writers tended to follow the rules of fair play, as laid out by Father Ronald Knox in 1929. These guidelines ruled out supernatural solutions, excess secret passageways, undiscovered poisons, and murderous twins. They also stipulated that the author must present the reader with all of the clues and must mention the criminal somewhere early in the story.

As the world slipped into a second global conflict, societal changes began to be reflected in the mystery stories. Although the cozy, manor house puzzle still attracted some readers, a new, harder-edged crime novel began to become popular. In the 1920s, Dashiell Hammett, a former Pinkerton agent, began publishing crime stories in the influential *Black Mask* magazine. These tales featured a more realistic approach to crime and looked to the urban streets for their inspiration. The body counts grew, and the language became rougher, as did the investigators. Hammett's *Red Harvest* (1929) was a hit, as were his follow-up novels *The Maltese Falcon* (1930) and *The Thin Man* (1934). Hammett led the way for other writers of hard-boiled crime fiction, including Raymond Chandler (*The Big Sleep,* 1939), Mickey Spillane (*I, the Jury,* 1947), and Ross Macdonald (*The Moving Target,* 1949).

During the 1950s and 1960s, mystery fiction continued to thrive, with hard-boiled PIs and cozies featuring amateur sleuths dominating the marketplace. There was little innovation during this period, with most writers relying on tried-and-true themes to carry the story. The puzzle mystery dominated the cozy side of the genre, and no big city was complete without at least a handful of private investigators living alcohol-sodden lives and using their fists and guns to bring justice to a chaotic world. The police procedural began to become popular, with its emphasis on teamwork rather than one supercop. Authors such as Hilary Waugh (*Last Seen Wearing,* 1952), Jonathan Craig (*The Dead Darling,* 1955), and J. J. Marric (*Gideon's Day,* 1955) introduced readers to the pleasures of following an investigation according to crime scene procedures.

In the 1970s and 1980s, societal changes once again influenced the development of the crime novel. The face of crime fiction began to look a bit more like the face of contemporary society. Moving women from the genteel investigator to the tough PI, Marcia Muller introduced Sharon McCone in *Edwin of the Iron Shoes* (1977), and Sue Grafton's Kinsey Millhone made her debut in *A Is for Alibi* (1982). Building on the earlier work of Chester Himes, the late 1980s saw the debut of such African American detectives as Gar Anthony Haywood's Aaron Gunner (*Fear of the Dark,* 1988). Investigations in the gay and lesbian communities were taken on by gay and lesbian detectives, with Joseph Hansen's *Fadeout* (1970) initiating the trend and Richard Stevenson's Donald Strachey expanding the role of the gay sleuth, *Death Trick* (1981). Some writers, like Sara Paretsky, used their crime novels to explore social concerns (*Indemnity Only,* 1982).

The 1990s saw an explosion in the popularity of crime fiction of all sorts. Although the mystery was still at the center of the story, frame elements like setting and time period became increasingly important. Historical mysteries offered readers the opportunity to explore other times, and mysteries with a strong sense of place took readers to locations that they might never visit. The details of the detectives' lives also became central to the story, with readers looking for character development in addition to a good plot. Mysteries popped up that featured interesting details on everything from horse racing to quilting to gardening, and readers flocked to these stories.

As we move into the first decade of the twenty-first century, we are in many ways seeing another golden age of mystery writing. This one offers fans of crime fiction an amazing variety of stories, from cozy to hard-boiled and beyond. It is a great time to be a mystery reader, so plunge ahead into the lists and track down a great crime novel or two for yourself.

How to Use This Book

There are a variety of ways that you can choose to use the lists in this book. You can, if you wish, start at the first one and read straight through, picking out titles that you might enjoy. If you have a particular reading preference or preferences, you can find the lists that reflect those interests and start there. Or you can open the book at random and plunge into the lists with abandon.

These lists are not intended to be comprehensive. There are so many mysteries out there that it would take reams of paper and gallons of ink to try and list all the possible titles in each category. Instead, the lists are intended to be jumping-off points for readers, offering some of the best examples of crime fiction arranged by their appeal. This structure has allowed the list compiler a lot of latitude. In any given list, you might find a cozy amateur sitting next to a hard-boiled PI. So there should be something in most of these lists that would appeal to any fan of crime and mystery fiction.

The lists are sorted alphabetically by author, and an arrow (⇨) next to a particular title indicates that this is a good starting point for the appeal associated with this list. The edition information given is, in most cases, for the most recent and available edition of the title. These will generally be paperback versions. If you prefer other editions, please check with your local library or bookseller to see what might be available.

The title annotations here intend to give you a brief plot summary and a sense of why this particular title is listed under this appeal factor. Many mystery titles are in series. The titles listed here are not always the first in the series, though they do always provide a good entry into the series. If you prefer to read series in order, your local librarian can assist you in getting a list of the author's titles in series order. The Kent District Library's "What's Next" Web site (http://www.kdl.org/libcat/WhatsNextNEW.asp) can also be a good resource for series information.

Chapter One

Story

At its core, any work of fiction is about the story. Story is perhaps the most basic appeal characteristic. It relates closely to the plot of the book: What are the elements of the tale? Is the emphasis more on the people or the situations? Is the story action focused or more interior? Is it funny? Scary? Are there special elements of the story that will attract readers and bring them back again and again to a particular author?

All crime fiction has a few basic story elements that draw the reader in. First there has to be a mystery. A crime is committed, and the reader follows along as the detective puzzles out the solution. Without this whodunit aspect, you do not really have a crime story. At the other end of the story, crime fiction generally does not leave the crime unsolved. Although there is not always a completely satisfying retribution dispensed, especially in more modern crime fiction, readers generally seek a sense that justice will prevail and good triumph over evil. If the criminal is not caught or otherwise incapacitated, many readers will feel a sense of incompleteness to the story.

Finally, crime fiction usually has a puzzle element that draws the reader into the story. Sometimes, the reader can solve the crime along with the detective, gathering the clues and coming to a conclusion about who the murderer was—the butler or the retired army colonel, that mousy-looking cousin or the bombshell with the checkered past. At other times, the reader is kept in the dark until the end, baffled by the red herrings strewn across the path. And then there are times where the person behind the crime is known from the beginning, and the story is more of a cat-and-mouse game between the detective and the criminal.

This chapter will give you a head start on finding crime stories to satisfy your interests, be they locked-room mysteries or police procedurals with lots of forensic detail. So pick up your scene-of-the-crime kit and cross the police tape and get to work.

It Must Be One of Us: Mysteries on Islands, Trains, and Other Isolated Locales

A classic mystery conceit gathers together a set of diverse characters, all apparently unconnected, in some lonely locale and then cuts them off from the outside world. Soon, bodies start appearing, and the ensemble realizes that there must be a killer in its midst. As the body count grows, so does the paranoia and the readers' enjoyment of the tension among the survivors. Snowbound manor houses and trains, isolated islands, and ships at sea all provide great locales for these stories.

Bryan, Kate
A Record of Death. **Maggie Maguire mysteries.** 1998. Berkley, ISBN 042516537X, 224p.

Bryan takes her plot to California in the 1870s. San Francisco private eye Maggie Maguire is stranded at a resort for wealthy Californians on Cutthroat Island (a name that doesn't bode well for the rest of the characters). As the threats to their fellow strandees mount up, Maggie and her chum, Grady, get to work to solve the mystery. Good historical detail and winning characters make this a fun, if light, mystery.

Christie, Agatha
⇨ *And Then There Were None.* 2001. St. Martin's Paperbacks, ISBN 1568497369, 288p.

When you think of a mystery with trapped characters and a mysterious killer, Christie is usually the first to come to mind. An unusual mixture of characters all receive invitations to come and visit a supposed acquaintance's home on an isolated island. Once they arrive, an unknown voice on a recording accuses them of avoiding prosecution for murder in the past, and the retribution begins. Christie's story combines thriller and mystery elements into a haunting story that many say is the best crime fiction ever written.

Daheim, Mary
Snow Place to Die. **Bed and Breakfast mysteries.** 1998. Avon, ISBN 0380785218, 304p.

Daheim takes her protagonist, bed-and-breakfast proprietor Judith Flynn, away from the homestead in this entry in the long-running series. Flynn is off to help her cousin cater a party at a mountain lodge, but a storm blows in and the guests and caterers are trapped. Following Judith's discovery of the body of last year's caterer, the killings begin again, and Judith and her cousin must find the killer before he finds them. This is an excellent cozy whodunit.

Gunning, Sally

Rough Water. **Peter Bartholomew mysteries.** 1994. Pocket, ISBN 0671871374, 304p.

New England settings and an affinity for watery plots mark Gunning's Peter Bartholomew series. *Rough Water* takes a new tack on the plotline, sending Bartholomew out on a whale-watching expedition with his sister and her unpleasant fiancé. A broken radio effectively isolates the group, the fiancé meets a speedy death on a harpoon, and Bartholomew steps in to find the killer.

Hart, Carolyn

Dead Man's Island. **Henrie O mysteries.** 1993. Bantam, ISBN 0553091735, 276p.

Noted mystery writer Hart introduced her detective, Henrietta O'Dwyer Collins, in this homage to Agatha Christie. A former lover asks Collins to find out who has been trying to kill him. He invites the suspects to his private island off the South Carolina coast, where surprising deaths and an approaching hurricane add to the tension and the excitement. Henrie O, as she is known to her friends, is a more acerbic Miss Marple, who uses logic to solve the puzzle.

James, P. D.

The Lighthouse. **Adam Dalgliesh mysteries.** 2006. Vintage, ISBN 0307275736, 400p.

A master of elegant, literary mystery stories, James's most recent entry hearkens back to the traditional mystery plot. Commander Dalgliesh and his team are dispatched to isolated Combe Island, off the Cornish coast, to investigate a killing. The island is run by a foundation as a place of respite for the powerful—politicians, writers, artists—and the initial investigation seems fairly commonplace, until another body is discovered. James's portrayals of her characters' lives and concerns are always exceptional.

Page, Katherine Hall

The Body in the Ivy. **Faith Fairchild mysteries.** 2006. William Morrow, ISBN 0060763655, 256p.

In another homage to Christie's *And Then There Were None*, Page brings a group of women college classmates to a remote island home. The homeowner, a top-selling mystery writer who is a fellow alumna, has invited them all. Page's detective, caterer Faith Fairchild, is brought in to organize food for the event but finds herself investigating mysterious deaths after a storm cuts off the island from the mainland.

An Artful Death: The Fine Arts and Crime

The art world offers a wonderful setting for crime fiction. All the elements are there—expensive objects, intercontinental intrigue, and a Byzantine world of characters who move from high society to the backstreets. The artists' egos, the jealousy between galleries and museums, and the backstabbing of the critics all offer possibilities for both victims and criminals. The books in this list explore various pieces of the art world, and together they create a fascinating portrait of the lives and deaths of the artists.

Dickinson, David

Death of an Old Master. **Lord Francis Powerscourt mysteries.** 2004. Carroll and Graf, ISBN 0786713062, 272p.

A scheme to sell forged copies of old master paintings results in the death of an art critic who was working on an essay that would call these works into question. Lord Powerscourt is drawn into the mystery and must delve into the shadowy world of art verification in late nineteenth-century England. The book is filled with details of the lives of the artists and techniques of forgery.

Henderson, Lauren

Strawberry Tattoo. **Sam Jones mysteries.** 2000. Three Rivers Press, ISBN 0609806858, 316p.

Henderson provides a peek into the contemporary art scene, complete with lots of alcohol, plenty of drugs (licit and otherwise), and an ample helping of sex. Sam Jones is an English sculptor who receives an invitation to participate in a group show at an upscale New York City gallery. Then a curator at the gallery is strangled and an exhibit vandalized, and Sam sets her sculpting tools aside to track down the killer. She's no Miss Marple though, and before things are settled Sam has to fight for her own life.

Laurence, Janet

Canaletto and the Case of the Westminster Bridge. 1998. Thomas Dunne Books, ISBN 0312185510, 393p.

Who better to uncover hidden secrets and murder than a painter? Robbed on his arrival in England in the 1740s, the Italian painter Canaletto is befriended by aspiring artist Fanny Rooker. In order to rescue Fanny from prison, Canaletto agrees to look into problems plaguing the completion of the Westminster Bridge. With an eye for detail and excellent powers of observation, the Italian artist unravels the mystery in a story filled with details of period art and craft.

Leon, Donna
Acqua Alta. **Guido Brunetti mysteries.** 2004. Penguin, ISBN 0142004960, 416p.

Part of her ongoing series set in Venice, Leon's police commissioner Brunetti is called in to investigate a theft of Chinese artifacts and the beating of archaeologist Brett Lynch. The plot expands, though, when the director of the local museum, who worked with Lynch on a display of Chinese artifacts in the past, is murdered. Brunetti finds himself drawn into the world of archaeological forgery and art theft.

Pears, Iain
⇨ *The Last Judgement*. **Jonathan Argyll and Flavia DiStefano mysteries.** 1999. Berkley, ISBN 0425171485, 288p.

Jonathan Argyll is a somewhat hapless art historian and occasional seller of paintings whose work brings him in touch with the seedy edges of the art community and frequently puts him in danger of imprisonment or worse. Fortunately, his friend (later wife) Flavia DiStefano is a member of the art-theft division of the Roman police force. In this installment of their story, Argyll is asked to deliver a painting from Paris to a dealer in Rome. This seemingly innocuous task results in several deaths, and the solution hinges on events during the German occupation of France in World War II.

Perez Reverte, Arturo
The Flanders Panel. 2004. Harvest Books, ISBN 0156029588, 304p.

Julia is an art restorer in Madrid who discovers a hidden message in a fifteenth-century painting that she is cleaning. The mysterious message leads her to investigate a questionable death of one of the painting's sitters, but at the same time her investigations touch off violence in her world. Perez Reverte's multilayered tale blends art, chess, and intrigue.

Sayers, Dorothy
Five Red Herrings. **Lord Peter Wimsey mysteries.** 1995. HarperTorch, ISBN 006104363X, 368p.

The Scottish village of Kirkcudbright is a haven for artists, and no one is too surprised when the irascible, hard-drinking painter Sandy Campbell is found at the bottom of the cliff where he had been painting. Is it an accident? Six other artists have all recently quarreled with Campbell, giving them possible motives for killing him. Peter Wimsey applies his usual intelligence to the case, as well as his analysis of painting techniques and styles and railroad timetables, and brings the case to a successful conclusion.

Swan Songs: Murder and Music

Like the art world, the music business offers mystery writers fertile ground for their stories. From classical to jazz to folk to rock, the music field seems to be populated by double-crossing agents, unscrupulous promoters, egotistical stars, and the occasional horn-playing detective. These books all leave you whistling (sometimes in the dark).

Duchin, Peter, and John Morgan Wilson
Good Morning Heartache. **Philip Damon mysteries.** 2004. Berkley, ISBN 0425199215. 304p.

It's 1965, and bandleader Philip Damon is bringing his big band out to LA for a gig at the Cocoanut Grove club. Fortunately, he has with him his sax player, Hercules Platt, who is a former cop. Damon is short a trumpeter and hires a replacement, but the new man is found dead of an apparent overdose. Damon and Platt delve into the LA music and glamour scene to unravel the mystery.

Frommer, Sara
The Vanishing Violinist. **Joan Spencer mysteries.** 2000. Worldwide Library, ISBN 0373263597, 256p.

An international violin competition brings a big crowd to Indianapolis, including the future son-in-law of Joan Spencer, manager of the local orchestra. Bad luck stalks the competitors, though, and a stolen Stradivarius and a missing violinist lead Joan to investigate the world of music competitions. Frommer captures the hectic and tension-filled life of a young classical performer, and she writes about music with rare skill.

Glatzer, Hal
Fugue in Hell's Kitchen. **Katy Green mysteries.** 2004. Daniel and Daniel, ISBN 1880284707, 240p.

Violins are not only played in classical music, and Glatzer's Katy Green is an accomplished swing player looking for work in New York City just before World War II. Investigating a stolen music manuscript for a friend leads Katy to the library of a music academy in Hell's Kitchen. As bodies turn up, Katy's investigation takes a darker turn and leads her across New York City from the jazz clubs to the conservatories. Glatzer gets the period and music details just right.

Grabien, Deborah
The Weaver and the Factory Maid. **English Ballad mysteries.** 2003. St. Martin's Minotaur, ISBN 0312314221, 192p.

The English folk-music scene is the setting for Grabien's series that mixes music, mystery, and the supernatural. Folk singer Ringan Laine comes into possession of a cottage in Somerset and quickly finds the property haunted by the ghosts of a pair of lovers who were killed in the early nineteenth century. The story uses the old ballad "The Weaver and the Factory Maid" as a jumping-off point for each chapter, as Laine and his musical friends uncover the story of the ill-fated lovers and put their spirits to rest.

Gur, Batya

➪ *Murder Duet: A Musical Case*. **Michael Ohayon mysteries.** 2000. Harper Paperbacks, ISBN 0060932988, 444p.

Israeli writer Batya Gur is known for creating thoughtful and driven Jerusalem Police Superintendent Michael Ohayon. In this case, Ohayon is drawn into the world of professional classical musicians when the husband and son of a cellist are murdered. The cellist is a close friend of Ohayon, and her family is deeply involved in music, both as performers and instrument dealers. Gur has a fine sense for the way music affects us and writes lyrically about music and musicians.

Holmes, Rupert

Swing. 2005. Random House, ISBN 140006158X, 384p.

Rupert Holmes may be known to most of us as the composer and performer of "The Piña Colada Song" in the late 1970s. But he is also a gifted writer, whose stage mysteries have won Edgar Awards. In *Swing,* Holmes takes us back to 1940 San Francisco, the heart of the swing era. Jazz musician Ray Sherwood comes to town with his band looking for gigs but finds murder and espionage in his way. Holmes has a keen sense of the life of the traveling musician, and the book is accompanied by a CD of Holmes's own swing compositions that relate to the tale.

Lopresti, Robert

Such a Killing Crime. 2005. Kearney Street Books, ISBN 0972370633, 262p.

Bob Dylan, Tom Paxton, Phil Ochs—it is 1963, and the folk scene in Greenwich Village is booming. Joe Talley manages the folk club The Riding Beggar, and when a promising singer is killed and his demo tapes stolen, Talley takes it on himself to track down the missing recordings and solve the crime. Lopresti has an ear and an eye for Village life in the 1960s, and his portrayals of the time and the people sing out.

Ross, Kate

The Devil in Music. **Julian Kestrel mysteries.** 1998. Penguin, ISBN 0140263640, 480p.

Where would opera and Italy be without each other? Passionate, extravagant, soulful, the opera world proves a wonderful setting for a mystery. Here, nineteenth-century dandy and sleuth Julian Kestrel must uncover the secrets surrounding the murder of a music-loving aristocrat, supposedly killed by an up-and-coming young singer. Ross's plot is as complex as a Verdi opera and has at least as many characters. From the famed La Scala theater to the homes of the Milanese aristocracy, Kestrel brings the mystery to a harmonious climax.

Deadly Hobbies: Or the Dangers of Quilting, Genealogy, and Gardening

We generally think of gardening, quilting, and the book trade as the provinces of gentle souls who would not hurt a fly (well, maybe a cabbage worm or two, but nothing more). So it is a shock to discover how much mayhem and murder seems to follow those who take up these peaceful pursuits. This list pulls together the best mysteries set in the world of arts and crafts.

Albert, Susan Wittig

⇨ *Love Lies Bleeding*. **China Bayles mysteries.** 1998. Berkley, ISBN 0425166112, 336p.

What could be more peaceful than running an herb shop? So it seems when China Bayles leaves her job as an attorney in Houston for the more relaxed pace of life in Pecan Springs. But bodies keep turning up in town, and China takes on the job of unearthing the killers. In this entry in the series, a Texas Ranger is dead, and the question is suicide or murder. Albert's stories are seasoned with herb lore, gardening tips, and interesting characters.

Dereske, Jo

Miss Zukas and the Library Murders. **Miss Zukas mysteries.** 2006. Avon, ISBN 038077030X, 272p.

Who can resist a mystery in which the librarian finds a body in the stacks that was killed by a catalog card drawer rod through the heart. Certainly this is a recommendation to convert to an online catalog. Miss Zukas normally finds herself dealing with little more than unruly patrons and the occasional lost book, but when she comes across that body, she takes on the task of making sure no one else is deaccessioned. Dereske captures the ups and downs of library work and introduces the reader to a host of quirky characters in the process.

Fowler, Earlene

Fool's Puzzle. **Benni Harper mysteries.** 1995. Berkley, ISBN 042514545X, 256p.

Benni Harper is a quilter and the curator of a small folk-art museum in California. It sounds like a quiet sort of life: stitching, putting up the occasional exhibit, and working with other artists in the community. But when a local potter is killed in the museum and Harper's cousin is a prime suspect, Benni has to step into the role of detective. Fowler includes information on the quilt pattern that gives each book in the series its title and crafts a tight mystery story.

Galligan, John

The Nail Knot. **Fly Fishing mysteries.** 2005. Bleak House Books, ISBN 1932557113, 264p.

Most hobby-centered mystery stories fall in the cozy category. The death is not too graphic, and the violence level and moral anguish are both pretty low. This is not the case with John Galligan's *The Nail Knot.* Ned Oglivie is a hard-drinking loner with a tragic past. But he is also a superb fly fisherman who lives to fish. When he discovers a body in a trout stream, he finds himself unwillingly caught up in solving the crime.

Harrison, Janis

Lilies that Fester. **Gardening mysteries.** 2002. St. Martin's Minotaur, ISBN 0312983174, 272p.

Florist Bretta Solomon's dead husband was a policeman, and Bretta finds that her involvement with crimes survives his passing. Having established a blossoming floral business, Bretta is off to Branson, Missouri, to help organize a florists' convention. Jealousies among the florists run high, though, and pretty soon its not just plants that end up in the ground. The series offers interesting garden and floral details and a mystery that keeps you reading.

King, Ross

Ex-Libris. 2002. Penguin, ISBN 0142000809, 400p.

King's historical mystery takes the reader back to the antiquaries of the seventeenth century. Isaac Inchbold, a bookseller on London Bridge, is hired to track down a missing book, stolen from a manor house library. More used to the sedentary life in his quiet store, Inchbold becomes caught up in dangerous adventures with more violent seekers of the book. King mixes politics, religion, and mystery in a complex and satisfying story. Bookselling is more dangerous than it appears.

MacPherson, Rett

Killing Cousins. **Torie O'Shea mysteries.** 2003. St. Martin's Minotaur, ISBN 0312983255, 256p.

Genealogists are always digging into the past, and sometimes they uncover unforeseen and unwanted details. When genealogist Torie O'Shea begins to research the family history of a local singer, she discovers a tragic story of a kidnapped child back in the 1930s. Demolition of the late singer's house uncovers the skeletal remains of a child, and a more recent killing has left a body at the same location. Torie puts together her researching and sleuthing skills to make the connections between the two apparently unrelated deaths.

Ripley, Ann

Death of a Political Plant. **Louise Eldridge mysteries.** 1998. Bantam Books, ISBN 0553577352, 308p.

Louise Eldridge has her hands full hosting a popular gardening show on PBS and keeping her own garden lush. Nonetheless, when a former boyfriend shows up needing a place to finish a piece of investigative journalism, she invites him into her house. His investigations are too close to the truth for someone, though, and he ends up as an unwelcome addition to a water garden. Louise and her CIA agent husband untangle the twisted political motives to solve the case. For avid gardeners, Ripley includes several essays on gardening topics interspersed with the mystery.

Playing with Death: Murder in the Sports World

Just like a good mystery story, a sporting event features a struggle between two people or teams. At the start, the outcome is unclear, but as they both progress, the conclusion becomes apparent in both mysteries and competitions. It is equally common that some twist occurs at the end. In sports, a Hail Mary pass is caught, a long putt is sunk, or a last burst of energy carries a long shot first across the finish line. In crime fiction, the likely criminal may turn out to be just another victim, or perhaps the butler really did do it. The sense of undetermined outcomes make the wide world of sports a great playing field for mystery writers. Here are some hall of fame stories.

Coben, Harlen
One False Move. **Myron Bolitar mysteries.** 1998. Delacorte Press, ISBN 0440225442, 322p.

> Coben takes on the world of sports through the eyes of sports agent Myron Bolitar. There seems to be as much sports action off the field as on, and Bolitar knows how to handle both sides of the game. In exchange for the opportunity to represent her, Bolitar agrees to keep an eye on the star of the women's basketball league, who has been receiving death threats. He finds that her problems center around her father, himself a noted athlete who has recently disappeared, and her long-gone mother.

Corrigan, John R.
Out of Bounds. **Jack Austin mysteries.** 2006. University Press of New England, ISBN 1584655852, 312p.

> Corrigan knows golf. Short game, irons, putting, he has it all down, and so does Jack Austin, Corrigan's pro golfing detective. In this outing, Austin is competing against more than the course as rumors of illegal performance enhancement are spreading on the tour. Soon, those suspected of using drugs to build their game start to die, and Austin tees off on the killer.

Evanovich, Janet
Motor Mouth. **Alexandra Barnaby mysteries.** 2006. HarperCollins, ISBN 0060834226, 304p.

Evanovich is best known for her smart-mouthed, funny heroines, and Alexandra Barnaby fits the mold. Barney, as she is known, grew up in her father's garage and knows cars and engines. So when her wayward lover, NASCAR driver Sam Hooker, ends up in second place and Barney suspects cheating, the action mounts up. Stolen cars, dead bodies, and some romance mix with fascinating NASCAR details.

Francis, Dick
⇨ *Dead Cert*. 2004. Berkley, ISBN 0425194973, 288p.

Horseracing is known as the sport of kings, but Francis's writing makes it accessible to everyone. No one better captures the senses and smells of the paddock, the stable, and the track. Francis's first novel, *Dead Cert,* centers around the death of a steeplechase jockey and a plot to throw races. Jockey Alan York takes on the task of uncovering the plot and avenging his friend's death.

Green, Tim
Double Reverse. 2000. Warner Books, ISBN 0446608491, 368p.

Having played eight years for the Atlanta Falcons, Tim Green knows the playbook on professional football. His characters' lives, on and off the field, reflect this understanding. In *Double Reverse,* an aspiring actress is killed, and the prime suspects are two teammates, each of whom had been involved with the victim. Lawyer and agent Madison McCall gets the call to defend one of the players and unmask the killer before time runs out on the field.

Hautman, Pete
The Prop. 2006. Simon and Schuster Paperbacks, ISBN 0743284658, 320p.

Props work to keep casino poker games going when they are short a player, receiving a salary from the casino but playing with their own money. Widow of a policeman, Patty Kane makes a living as a prop for a Native American casino in Arizona, and things are going pretty well for her. Then a robbery at the casino turns bloody, and Kane must investigate the crime to clear herself of suspicion. Hautman deals readers a winning hand here, with lots of card-playing detail.

McEvoy, John
Riders Down. 2006. Poisoned Pen Press, ISBN 1590582586, 120p.

McEvoy's 33 years as an editor and correspondent for the *Daily Racing Form* are clearly on display in his racing mysteries. His stories capture the tension and stress that thoroughbred racing brings to both animals and humans. Here, his journalism background is put to good use as well, as Matt O'Connor, a racing journalist, investigates a race-fixing scheme that takes him across the country and to a final confrontation with the villain behind the conspiracy.

Muller, Eddie

The Distance. **Billy Nichols mysteries.** 2002. Scribner, ISBN 0743214439, 304p.

Known as "the sweet science," boxing is really anything but. It is a violent world, frequently associated with the Mob and criminality. Muller, whose father was a noted boxing journalist, re-creates the seedy gyms and questionable characters of the world of boxing in the post–World War II era. Celebrated fight reporter Billy Nichols steps in to help a boxer who has accidentally (??) killed his manager. A definite noir knockout.

Parker, Robert B.

Playmates. **Spenser mysteries.** 1990. Berkley, ISBN 0425120015, 288p.

Parker's hero, Spenser, frequently finds himself working the edges of the sporting life. Spenser combines a sense of righteousness with a soft spot for those down on their luck. He is called in to investigate a point-shaving scandal in college basketball, and rather than take the easy route and accuse the player, Spenser keeps digging to bring those behind the scheme to justice. It is a fast-paced story that plays hard at both ends of the court.

Murder on the Front: Military Mysteries

It has been said that the battlefield is the perfect place to hide the results of a murder, there among all the other corpses. With the breakdown of social codes in wartime, crime can become rampant, both at the front and back home. It may be crimes against civilians or against soldiers who are in a strange country not of their own choosing. All the titles in this list depict the search for truth and justice in the midst of the violence and disorder that are the characteristics of war.

Baron, Aileen

A Torch of Tangier. 2006. Poisoned Pen Press, ISBN 1590582217, 194p.

Lily Sampson is an archaeologist who is working on a dig in Morocco in 1942. The city of Tangier is rife with plots and subplots, as the Allies begin planning the invasion of North Africa. Lily becomes involved in the operation while working for the OSS, but soon friends are killed, and she is worried that she may be next. The story is gripping, with interesting details of World War II on the North African front.

Claudel, Philippe

By a Slow River. 2006. Knopf, ISBN 1400042801, 208p.

Near a small French village, World War I rages, with hundreds of young men dying every day. But the concerns of the villagers are more often with their day-to-day existence. That seeming peace is shattered by the discovery of the body of a young girl who has been murdered, followed by the suicide of the local schoolteacher. The story is told as a reflection by the police officer who investigated the crime, as he thinks back on the choices that he made and the concern that a single death raised in the village when only a few miles away many more people were dying, unconsidered, every day.

James, Benn
Billy Boyle. 2006. Soho Press, ISBN 1569474338, 304p.

Billy Boyle is a newly minted policeman just like his dad and uncles, but World War II is heating up and he enlists. Family ties get Billy attached to Eisenhower's staff in London, where his first assignment is to uncover a spy. The task leads to Billy's investigation of the supposed suicide of a member of the Norwegian government in exile that could jeopardize the Allied invasion of Norway. James mixes romance, history, and military detail into a satisfying puzzle.

Janes, J. Robert
⇨ *Kaleidoscope*. **Jean-Louis St. Cyr and Hermann Kohler mysteries.** 2001. Soho Press, ISBN 1569472866, 294p.

Janes has crafted a fascinating series featuring an unlikely pair of detectives, Jean-Louis St. Cyr of the Paris Sûreté and Hermann Kohler of the Gestapo. Set in occupied France, the stories are filled with a sense of danger and despair that is at the heart of military occupation. This installment finds the pair sent to Provence to investigate the murder of a woman who was involved with the black market and possibly working with the Resistance. The two men are torn by their loyalties to their respective governments and to each other before the killer is uncovered.

McMillan, Ann
Angel Trumpet. **Civil War mysteries.** 2001. Penguin, ISBN 014029838X, 256p.

Virginia is torn by Civil War, with Union troops moving on Richmond. A white widow, Narcissa Powers, and a free black herbalist, Judah Daniel, are working as nurses at a Richmond hospital. In nearby Goochland, a Confederate colonel, on leave from his regiment, arrives home to find his family slain, apparently at the hands of their slaves. Powers and Daniel are called on to look into the killings. A finely drawn portrait of life in wartime with overtones of the racial issues that brought the United States to civil war.

Parry, Owen
Faded Coat of Blue. **Abel Jones mysteries.** 2000, Avon, ISBN 0380797399, 368p.

Abel Jones was wounded at the first battle of Manassas while fighting for the Union Army. Jones, a Welshman by birth, worries that the disgrace of the defeat at Manassas and his injury have consigned him to a desk job in Washington; however, a call from the headquarters of Union General McClellan gives Jones a chance for redemption. A popular Union officer, who is a strong abolitionist, has been murdered, and it is up to Jones to find the killer. Owen Parry's writing is highly descriptive, and his depictions of war and battle are chillingly real.

Perkins, Wilder
Hoare and the Portsmouth Atrocities. **Bartholomew Hoare mysteries.** 1998. St. Martin's Minotaur, ISBN 0312192835, 224p.

Wilder Perkins takes up the naval side of military crime during the Napoleonic period. Bartholomew Hoare was wounded in action, taking a musket ball in the throat, which left him incapable of speaking above a hoarse whisper. He can no longer continue as a captain in her majesty's navy and is relegated to the staff of a port admiral. Hoare is called on to investigate an apparently unconnected series of attacks and deaths. Perkins is steeped in British naval lore, and the books will satisfy old salts as well as mystery readers.

The Mystery of Terror

In the last decades of the twentieth century, terrorism, sadly, became part of the common knowledge of society. In the United States, the acts of September 11, 2001, brought this home in a most horrific fashion. It is common for reading trends to follow cultural trends, and in the same period mystery writers began to explore the shadowy worlds of domestic and international terrorism, and in some writers' works detectives can as often be found pursuing terrorists as chasing more quotidian criminals. This list comprises some of the writers who best capture the moral choices made by people on both sides of the question. These stories often combine elements of suspense with the unraveling of a puzzle.

Anderson, Jack, and Robert Westbrook
The Saudi Connection. 2006. Forge Books, ISBN 0765311445, 288p.

The posthumous work of muckraking journalist Jack Anderson, *The Saudi Connection* is a fast-paced, action-filled tale of a journalist, Ron Wright, whose career seems over after he is forced to give back a Pulitzer Prize for unknowingly writing a story based on false evidence. He gets a tip on a new story: The Saudis are rumored to have been funding a white supremacist organization in the United States, to the tune of $20 million. Soon the tipster is dead, and Ron is traveling to the Middle East to track down the killer and uncover the story.

Estleman, Loren
Nicotine Kiss. **Amos Walker mysteries.** 2006. Forge Books, ISBN 0765312239, 256p.

Amos Walker is a hard-boiled private eye in Detroit. He is working a simple tracking job, when he is shot in the leg. A small-time smuggler and sometime friend gets Amos to the hospital in time to save his life, but then the friend disappears. A federal agent warns Amos off trying to locate his rescuer, intimating that the smuggling is really a front for funding a terrorist organization. Amos persists though, flaunting Homeland Security and risking his own life in search of the truth.

Ford, Clyde

Deuce's Wild. **Shango mysteries.** 2006. Midnight Ink, ISBN 0738708097, 306p.

When rapper Deuce F, a recent convert to Islam, is shot outside a club in New York City, the police write it off as another hip-hop vendetta. But John Shannon, formerly of the NYPD, now working for the Office of Municipal Security, investigates. He discovers that Deuce had possible connections to violent Islamic fundamentalists within New York's Muslim community. Shannon's investigations become more dangerous the deeper he digs.

Keating, H.R.F.

One Man and His Bomb. **Harriet Martens mysteries.** 2006. St. Martin's Minotaur, ISBN 0312349882, 224p.

Keating's story opens with the death of one of Detective Superintendent Harriet Martens's sons in a London terrorist bombing. Her other son is badly injured. Despite her losses, Martens comes back to work and is given the assignment of tracking the theft of a hazardous herbicide that could be the next weapon for the terrorists. With its chilling portrayal of both international and domestic terror groups, Keating's book is a strong addition to the field.

Lock, Joan

Dead Loss. 2006. Severn House, ISBN 0727863118, 185p.

The weapon of terror is not entirely new to the late twentieth century. In the 1880s, London experienced a series of bomb attacks by the Irish nationalist Fenians. Police Detective Ernest Best is assigned to go undercover to infiltrate the Fenians and stop the next attacks. The job takes him to Paris and back to London, where he is also caught up in tracing a disappearance that may or may not be related to the bombings.

Mahoney, Dan

Once In, Never Out. **Brian McKenna mysteries.** 1998. St. Martin's Press, ISBN 0312182287, 352p.

IRA-related bombings are at the center of this entry in Mahoney's realistic and dark Brian McKenna series. McKenna is an NYPD detective who is called in to investigate the disappearance of the sister of a priest in the diocese of New York. The case takes him to Iceland, where he makes the connections between the missing girl and a plot to bomb the Saint Patrick's Day parade in New York City. The Irish "Troubles" are convincingly portrayed as McKenna tries to stop the bomber.

Silva, Daniel
⇨ *The Kill Artist*. **Gabriel Allon mysteries.** 2000. Random House, ISBN 0375500901, 448p.

No one captures the moral dilemmas involved in dealing with terror better than Daniel Silva. His Gabriel Allon novels are studies in moral complexity. In *The Kill Artist,* Allon, an art restorer and retired Israeli agent, is persuaded to come out of retirement to eliminate a rogue Palestinian assassin who is planning to kill Yasir Arafat. Silva has a strong sense of the difficulties that are faced by those engaged in tracking down terrorists, in terms of tactics and ethics.

Social Dis-eases: Detectives with a Conscience

Just as terrorism is an increasingly common story device in contemporary mysteries, social issues are also making their way onto the pages of crime fiction. Rather than tracking down a single individual for a crime, detectives now find themselves up against corrupt corporations, suspect government bureaucracies, and shady organizations. Although the actual killers may still be the objects of pursuit, it is their faceless masters who are the real targets of the investigations. Crime fiction authors are also using their stories to explore difficult social issues, such as divorce, family violence, and substance abuse.

Barnes, Linda
Snapshot. **Carlotta Carlyle mysteries.** 1993. Delacorte Press, ISBN 0385306121, 325p.

Hospitals and counterfeit pharmaceuticals are at the center of this entry in Linda Barnes's Carlota Carlyle series. A private investigator, Carlyle is asked to investigate the death of a child at a prestigious Boston hospital. The child had been receiving treatment for leukemia and all of a sudden took a turn for the worse and died. Now her mother is distraught, convinced that the hospital is responsible. Carlyle has to deal with the arrogance of the hospital staff, some of whom have something to hide, as she uncovers the truth about the girl's death.

D'Amato, Barbara
Hard Luck. **Cat Marsala mysteries.** 1992. Scribner, ISBN 0684194082, 242p.

Cat Marsala is an investigative reporter and finds her stories in the cesspool of greed and corruption that is Chicago politics. Here, Cat is on her way to interview a staff member of the Illinois lottery. He had contacted her about possible embezzlement of lottery funds. Unfortunately, he takes a long drop from the window of his office before Cat can catch up with him. Cat must take on the legalized gambling community to uncover the truth behind this death.

Haddam, Jane

Hardscrabble Road. **Gregor Demarkian mysteries.** 2006. St. Martin's Minotaur, ISBN 0312353731, 320p.

Haddam's detective is former FBI agent Gregor Demarkian, by all accounts a decent and upright man. In this installment, Demarkian is called on to look into the disappearance of a homeless man, who was purportedly acquiring drugs for a right-wing radio talk host (sound familiar?). The radio host enters rehab, but the homeless man, who was suing the host for defamation, winds up in the morgue. The motivations and machinations of the left, the right, politicians, and the Catholic Church all come into question in this moving story.

Maron, Margaret

Uncommon Clay. **Deborah Knott mysteries.** 2004. Mysterious Press, ISBN 089296720X, 272p.

Maron's Judge Deborah Knott stories are as much about the people of the North Carolina Piedmont and their lives as they are about the solving of a mystery, though Maron crafts a fine puzzle as well. Here, Judge Knott is involved in settling a divorce between two well-respected potters. When one of the parties is murdered, Judge Knott delves into the increasingly tangled and dark family ties that brought about the death. Maron is known for her sympathetic portrayal of the challenges of family relationships.

Muller, Marcia

Dead Midnight. **Sharon McCone mysteries.** 2002. Mysterious Press, ISBN 089296765X, 320p.

Sharon McCone is one of the original tough female private eyes. In this entry in the series, McCone tries to discover the truth behind the suicide of an employee at a hot new online magazine. At the same time, she is still suffering the effects of the suicide of her own brother. Her digging uncovers shady business practices and financial malfeasance at high levels as well as disturbingly unpleasant office politics. The effect of suicide on the survivors and the seamy side of the business world are equally featured here.

Paretsky, Sara

⇨ *Fire Sale.* **V. I. Warshawski mysteries.** 2005. Putnam, ISBN 0399152792, 416p.

Sara Paretsky's PI, V. I. Warshawski, has had to face down the shipping industry, the mob, entertainment moguls, and the Catholic Church. When V. I. comes back to her old neighborhood to coach the girl's basketball team at her old Chicago high school, she also begins to investigate a case of industrial sabotage and the disappearance of a young man. Both cases center around a large, family-operated discount merchant that controls most of the employment in the neighborhood. Paretsky uses V. I.'s investigation to explore the contrast between rich and poor and the treatment of low-wage workers by large companies.

Sherer, Michael
Death Is No Bargain. **Emerson Ward mysteries.** 2006. Five Star, ISBN 1594143684, 368p.

> Abortion, unwanted pregnancy, and the shadowy world of illicit adoption all come under scrutiny in Michael Sherer's latest Emerson Ward mystery. When a teenage girl runs away, Ward finds himself under fire for having sheltered her after an earlier incident. The girl turns up dead near a convent that takes in unwed mothers, and Ward goes undercover to scrutinize the activities of the sisters. Ward is also dealing with his girlfriend's pregnancy and the new responsibilities he feels toward their unborn child.

Spiegelman, Peter
Death's Little Helpers. **John March mysteries.** 2005. Knopf, ISBN 1400040795, 352p.

> The world of Wall Street and its financial misdoings is the locale for Spiegelman's latest. John March is well-off, supported by a family trust and raised in a family of financial wizards. He took the road less traveled, though, and chose to set up shop in New York City as a private eye. Here he is hired to find Gregory Danes, a Wall Street financier whose disappearance has left his divorced wife in desperate financial straits. Spiegelman knows Wall Street from his time in the finance industry, and he adeptly captures the dark side of finance.

Show Me the Money:
The Big Heists

Who can resist a really big robbery? Whether it is knocking over an armored car delivery, taking millions from a bank, or scamming the Mob (think of Paul Newman and Robert Redford in *The Sting*), the lure of going from poor to rich in a single stroke is a strong one for criminals and for mystery authors as well. The big-money stories usually either come at it from the criminal side—putting together the team and carrying out the robbery—or from the investigation side—tracking down that team and finding the stolen loot. Here are some of the biggest heists in crime fiction.

Austin, Ray
The Eagle Heist. **Beauford Sloan mysteries.** 2002. McKenna, ISBN 0971365946, 208p.

> An armored truck is hijacked, diamonds are missing, and all that can be found are the guards' bodies. The case seems destined for the cold files, until the mother of one of the guards hires PI Beauford Sloan to investigate. In short order, Sloan locates the missing truck, but now he is caught between the thieves and the federal investigators. A trip to Europe and North Africa lets Sloan tie together the disparate threads of the mystery.

Burton, Milton

The Sweet and the Dead. 2006. St. Martin's Minotaur, ISBN 0312343108, 272p.

We are in Biloxi in the early 1970s, and a loose group of bad good old boys, the Dixie Mafia, is planning a big caper. What they do not know is that the man that they have put in charge of rounding up the team is in fact working undercover for the police. Retired Sheriff Manfred "Hog" Webern left the force under murky circumstances, so the bad guys accept him as one of their own. But Webern finds he can't trust anyone as he tries to come out of the heist alive.

Connelly, Michael

Lost Light. **Harry Bosch mysteries.** 2003. Little, Brown, ISBN 0316154601 368p.

LAPD detective Harry Bosch is retired now, but he cannot let rest a cold case. While investigating the murder of a film production assistant, Bosch was on a movie set when robbers hijacked an armored car with millions in it, intended to be used in a film scene. But both cases ended in the cold files. A call from one of the officers originally involved in the cases spurs Bosch to sort through the connections between the two crimes, and his investigations lead him to a confrontation with the FBI. Bosch follows the money to bring the case to a conclusion.

Crichton, Michael

The Great Train Robbery. 2002. Avon, ISBN 0060502304, 352p.

One of the twists you may find in a caper or heist story is to follow the crime through the eyes of the criminal. Crichton tells of a plot to steal a military payroll as it is transported across England via train. The pleasure in the story comes from seeing how the mastermind, Edward Pierce, puts together his gang and acquires the necessary keys to unlock the safe (four are needed, all held by different people). The story is based on the 1855 robbery of the South Eastern Railway.

Holton, Hugh

The Devil's Shadow. **Larry Cole mysteries.** 2001. Forge, ISBN 0312877846, 382p.

Chicago seems to have more than its share of big heists, but the target is not always cash or jewels. *The Devil's Shadow,* featuring Chicago Chief of Detectives Larry Cole, begins with the theft of a videotape and a gun from the vaults of the Metropolitan Bank of Chicago. The items were wanted by Mob boss Jake Romano, as they implicated him in the killing of another mobster. Romano has brought in the infamous, and highly successful, thief "The Devil's Shadow" to pull off the job and to set up a second bank job that will give him needed capital. Cole and his team confront the mob, the thief, and a host of other dangerous characters.

Phillips, Gary

High Hand. **Martha Chainey mysteries.** 2000. Kensington Books, ISBN 1575666162, 241p.

There are easier and safer jobs than being a courier for the mob, but that is what Martha Chainey has chosen to do. Unfortunately for her, on her latest job, delivering $7 million to a Vegas casino, she is set up, a bunch of folks die, and the money is stolen. She now has three days to get the money back or face the consequences. Not your usual caper tale, but Phillips manages to make Chainey a sympathetic character as she tries to track down the killers and save her own life. Phillips writes with a very noir feel, with lots of violence and sex.

Stark, Richard

⇨ *The Man with the Getaway Face*. **Parker mysteries.** 1984. Allison and Busby, ISBN 0446674664, 155p.

Stark's protagonist is the violent, though dispassionate, criminal Parker. Parker is on the run and has plastic surgery both to cover his tracks and to prepare for his next scheme: an armored car robbery. Stark excels at taking someone you would not necessarily want to meet and somehow turning him into a more or less appealing character. The book is filled with the meticulous planning of the heist, but, as often happens, the best laid plans fail, and Parker is left to deal with the aftermath.

Vachss, Andrew

The Getaway Man. 2003. Vintage, ISBN 1400031192, 192p.

The big heist was a staple of pulp crime fiction in the 1950s. Vachss hearkens back to those days with his stand-alone story of a troubled young man with a love of fast cars. Eddie has been in and out of detention since his childhood, but his skills as a driver attract the attention of J. C., who is planning that big heist that will mean he can retire. Eddie is an appealing antihero, and Vachss's writing is as sparkling and cold as a load of diamonds.

Grand Complications: Twisty Plots and Complex Stories

Sometimes you really want a crime story that reaches beyond the usual plot in which a crime is committed, investigation follows, and the criminal is brought to justice. If you have a yearning for plots filled with twists and turns, multilayered storytelling, and a complex cast of characters and motivations, then the titles listed here should all provide satisfaction. These are stories that you can sink deeply into, coming up for air only when necessary.

Akunin, Boris
Murder on the Leviathan. **Erast Fandorin mysteries.** 2005. Random House, ISBN 0812968794, 240p.

Although not quite as complicated as Dostoyevsky, Akunin's series, set in czarist Russia and featuring diplomat and detective Erast Fandorin, does offer a plethora of Russian names to remember and a plot that resembles one of those nesting dolls, in which each new discovery contains surprises. The plot centers on the brutal murder of a British aristocrat and his family in France. The French police believe the killer is headed to India on the steamship *Leviathan,* and Fandorin steps in to assist.

Cleverly, Barbara
The Bee's Kiss. **Detective Joe Sandilands mysteries.** 2007. Delta, ISBN 0385340419, 352p.

It seemed like a jewel theft gone wrong when the body of Dame Beatrice Joliffe is found at London's Ritz Hotel. But Scotland Yard Commander Joe Sandilands, just back from a stint in India, suspects there is more to the killing. He is right, and the plot spirals deep into political corruption and blackmail in the British military. Cleverly captures 1920s England, and the her plot and characters will keep you enthralled.

Grimes, Martha
The Five Bells and Bladebone. **Richard Jury mysteries.** 2002. Onyx, ISBN 0451410386, 352p.

Grimes is notable for her leisurely paced plots that mix suspense and humor. She introduces new twists in every chapter and excels at connecting the disparate stories in the end. Here, Inspector Jury's investigation of a local murder is complicated by the discovery of a second killing that seems to be related to the first. It's up to you and Jury to figure out how in this oblique tale.

Kurzweil, Alan
➪ *The Grand Complication*. 2002. Hyperion, ISBN 0786885181, 368p.

This sprawling literary mystery is as complicated as the clockwork of the eighteenth-century timepiece that gives the book its name. A superb reference librarian is hired by an eccentric collector to locate a missing piece from a cabinet of curiosities. Pop-up books, Marie Antoinette, hidden compartments, lettering, and more are all part of the mystery and the literary thrills here.

Rankin, Ian
Dead Souls. **Inspector Rebus mysteries.** 2000. St. Martin's Paperbacks, ISBN 0312974205, 448p.

As you would guess from the inspector's name, Rankin's series offers complex layers of meaning. Like many police procedurals, the story here is not limited to a single plotline but reflects the myriad cases that police are dealing with, often simultaneously. Rebus's personal troubles and a multitude of difficult cases—vigilantism, a disappearance, the suicide of a colleague, child abuse—almost overwhelm the inspector. But Rankin pulls all the lines together in a satisfying, if dark, conclusion.

Robinson, Peter
Strange Affair. **Inspector Banks mysteries.** 2006. Avon, ISBN 0060544341, 416p.

Inspector Alan Banks left London in hopes of finding a more peaceful existence in northern England. But he discovers that the rural Yorkshire countryside can be just as dark and violent as the big city. In this multilayered tale, Banks searches for his disappeared brother while one of his officers is investigating a murder in which the victim had Banks's address in her pocket. These investigations twist around one another in an increasingly complex spiral.

Tapply, William
Gray Ghost. **Stoney Calhoun mysteries.** 2007. St. Martin's Minotaur, ISBN 0312363036, 272p.

Both the characters and the story are intricate and shadowed in Tapply's latest title. Stoney Calhoun is now a Maine fishing guide, whose past was erased from his memory by a lightening strike. Throughout the story, bits of his past rise to the surface and tantalizingly disappear again. The plot, involving murder and vigilantism seemingly rooted in the past, grows equally complex as Calhoun assists the local sheriff in solving the case.

Van de Wetering, Janwillem
Hard Rain. **Grijpstra and de Gier mysteries.** 1997. Soho Crime, ISBN 1569471045, 313p.

The Amsterdam murder squad is home to some of the most complicated policemen that you will ever meet. Van de Wetering's characters mix Zen Buddhism, a love for jazz music, and problematic love lives, as well as a host of twisty cases told in a stream-of-consciousness style that adds another layer. Here, the squad investigates the murder of a Dutch banker and the apparently linked deaths of three addicts.

Youthful Indiscretions: Mysteries for the Young Reader

I still remember the enjoyment I took as a child in reading mystery stories. Often of the puzzle variety, these tales of crimes, sometimes petty and sometimes serious, laid the groundwork for my continued interest in crime fiction of all sorts. Listed below is some of the best crime fiction for the young and the young at heart, both classics and newer authors.

Balliett, Blue
Chasing Vermeer. 2005. Scholastic Paperbacks, ISBN 0439372976, 272p.

　　If you like puzzles of all sorts, then Balliett's delightful contemporary mystery set in Chicago should appeal to you. Two sixth-grade girls become fast friends as they try to solve a series of puzzles that will lead them to a stolen Vermeer painting. Balliett puts the puzzles on the page for the reader to solve if you want to test your skills.

Bellairs, John
The Curse of the Blue Figurine. **Johnny Dixon and Professor Childermass mysteries.** 2004. Puffin, ISBN 0142402583, 208p.

　　Bellairs offers an enchanting mix of eerie suspense and mystery in most of his juvenile titles. Here, the professor and Johnny must solve the mystery of a figurine that Johnny finds in his church. Ancient Egyptian curses and strange happenings follow in the figurine's wake.

Byars, Betsy Cromer
⇨ *The Dark Stairs*. **Herculeah Jones mysteries.** 1997. Puffin, ISBN 0140369961, 160p.

　　With a policeman father and a PI mother, you would expect 13-year-old Herculeah Jones to be an expert sleuth. Here, she investigates the mysteries surrounding an old mansion. Great characters and a good blend of mystery and suspense make this an excellent series.

Colfer, Eoin
Half Moon Investigations. 2006. Miramax, ISBN 0786849576, 304p.

　　Best known for his Artemis Fowl series, Colfer here starts a new cycle featuring 12-year-old Fletcher Moon. Armed with a PI license that he got over the Internet, Moon takes on investigations in his Irish hometown. Readers will find Colfer's unique mix of wit and clever characters on display here.

Dixon, Franklin
The Tower Treasure. **Hardy Boys mysteries.** 1976. Grosset and Dunlap, ISBN 0448089017, 180p.

　　Decades after their first appearance, Frank and Joe Hardy still offer young readers thrills and adventures. In this debut story in the series, the dynamic sons of investigator Fenton Hardy investigate a mystery surrounding a stolen car and a jewel theft from the mysterious Tower Mansion in their hometown of Bayport.

Keene, Carolyn
The Secret of the Old Clock. **Nancy Drew mysteries.** 1991. Applewood Books, ISBN 1557091552, 210p.

　　Like the Hardy Boys, Nancy Drew and her pals have been on the case a long time, but the thrill is still there for those who enjoy intrepid female detectives. Here, Nancy and her father investigate a missing will and a stolen clock. The solution results in a large legacy going to the rightful heirs.

Sobol, Donald J.
Encyclopedia Brown, Boy Detective. **Encyclopedia Brown mysteries.** 1985. Yearling, ISBN 0553157248, 128p.

    In another case of a son taking after his father, Leroy "Encyclopedia" Brown, son of Idaville's police chief, sets up his own detective agency and sets about solving crimes. These are classic puzzle mysteries, and Sobol leaves it up to the reader to solve the crime along with Encyclopedia. He thoughtfully puts the solutions in the back of the book.

Van Draanen, Wendelin
Sammy Keyes and the Hotel Thief. **Sammy Keyes mysteries.** 1998. Yearling, ISBN 0679892648, 176p.

    Thirteen-year-old Samantha Keyes secretly lives with her grandmother in a retirees-only apartment. When she witnesses a robbery at the next-door hotel, she can't call the police, because they would take her away from her grandmother, so she sets out to solve the crime herself. A fine series, featuring a spunky female lead.

Death by Chocolate (or Other Culinary Delights): Crime and Cooking

    The combination of murder and haute cuisine seems a little disturbing on the surface. But when you think about it, crime fiction that centers around food and eating makes sense. There are lots of folks gathered together for a meal, giving an ample supply of suspects. The food connection offers opportunity to explore a variety of poisons. And, perhaps most important, readers really seem to enjoy these culinary mysteries. All of the titles in this list use the language of food to great effect, and most of them include recipes for the reader to try, if you dare.

Childs, Laura
The English Breakfast Murder. **Tea Shop mysteries.** 2003. Berkley, ISBN 042519129X, 288p.

    If the Japanese raised tea drinking to an art, Laura Childs has made that art all her own in this cozy series featuring tea shop owner Theodosia Browning and her stalwart staff. The stories are steeped in the lore and language of tea, and drinking and eating play a central role. Here, Browning turns up the body of a local art and antique dealer, and there are a host of candidates for role of murderer. The back matter includes a dozen recipes for dishes mentioned in the book.

Conant-Park, Jessica, and Susan Conant
  Steamed. **Gourmet Girls mysteries.** 2006. Berkley, ISBN 0425208052, 304p.
    This mother-and-daughter team pair up to provide a delicious mystery. The story stars reluctant graduate student and food aficionado Chloe Carter getting her degree in social work in Boston. Chloe lives for food, and when a blind date goes wrong (he turns up dead), she takes up the investigation. The authors cook up a delectable mix of food, mystery, and romance with recipes.

Davidson, Diane Mott
  ➪ *Tough Cookie*. **Goldy Schultz mysteries.** 2001. Bantam, ISBN 0553578308, 336p.
    Davidson has been serving up fresh mysteries featuring caterer Goldy Schultz since the early 1990s that mix interesting food writing, crime, and recipes. In this entry, Goldy is temporarily out of work due to plumbing problems and takes the offer to host a TV food show. In a Rachel Raye meets Kinsey Millhone mash-up, Goldy turns from the kitchen to the crime scene when bodies begin turning up.

Fluke, Joann
  Chocolate Chip Cookie Murder. **Hannah Swenson mysteries.** 2001. Kensington, ISBN 0758215053, 336p.
    Readers with a sweet tooth will devour Fluke's series set in small-town Minnesota and featuring baker and coffee shop owner Hannah Swenson. Baked goods are at the center of the story, and Fluke liberally sprinkles in cookie recipes. The mystery begins when Swenson finds her dairy delivery man shot behind her store. This series is as comfortable and cozy as a good cookie and a glass of milk.

King, Peter
  Eat, Drink, and Be Buried. **Gourmet Detective mysteries.** 2004. St. Martin's Minotaur, ISBN 0312980132, 240p.
    The nameless protagonist of this series has given up a career as a high-level chef to become a culinary detective, tracking down lost recipes and unique ingredients. Here, he is hired to re-create medieval menus for an English estate's theme restaurant, but when the bodies start dropping, he takes on the investigation. A former chef himself, King writes lovingly and lyrically about food.

MacInerney, Karen
  Murder on the Rocks. **Gray Whale Inn mysteries.** 2006. Midnight Ink, ISBN 0738709085, 282p.
    Running a bed and breakfast can be a tenuous existence, and Natalie Barnes is not as successful as she had hoped, despite her mouthwatering cooking for

the few guests who have checked in. Then there is the concern over development of the Maine island where her B&B is located. When the developer ends up at the bottom of the cliff, dead, Barnes puts down her spatula and takes up the case. MacInerney has a great feel for writing about food, and the recipes are delightful.

Myers, Tamar

The Crepes of Wrath. **Magdalena Yoder mysteries.** 2002. Signet, ISBN 0451203224, 272p.

The Pennsylvania Dutch are known for their plain but delicious cookery, and that reputation is on display in Myers's series featuring mouthwatering recipes from the kitchen of Mennonite innkeeper, and sometime detective, Magdalena Yoder. A poisoned batch of crepes has carried off a member of Yoder's community, and the sheriff deputizes Yoder to take on the case. The series mixes humor and food into a hearty, if not gourmet, meal.

Temple, Lou Jane

Death du Jour. **Spice Box mysteries.** 2006. Berkley, ISBN 0425208060, 272p.

In a unique take on the culinary mystery, Temple sets her series in various historical periods. A restaurateur, Temple has a great command of the language of food as well as a sense of history and blends the two into a delightful confection. This entry is set in Revolutionary France and features Fanny Delarue, cook for a wealthy family. When the family flees the Terror, Fanny is left behind and finds herself in trouble with the police and an unknown murderer. Interesting recipes for historical foods offer a new taste in culinary crime fiction.

Chapter Two

Character

For many readers, character is the most important element of a story, be it a mystery, a romance, or a work of literary fiction. As readers, we respond to different character types at different times. Sometimes you want the comfort of meeting old friends and renewing their acquaintance. Hence the popularity of series characters in crime fiction. There is something very appealing about coming to a new story with characters that you already know. They may be tough-guy PIs or perhaps clever old lady detectives or anywhere in between, but we readers of crime fiction take pleasure in seeing what these familiar companions are up to now.

Like most genres, crime writing has its share of stock characters: the mobster with a heart of gold, the hard-pressed and overworked police detective, the amateur investigator with an independent income, and the busybody old lady all come to mind. Over the course of a series, though, these characters frequently grow and develop new facets. These changes have a strong appeal for readers as well.

At other times, you might want to explore new character types, leaving the familiar behind and trying out something a bit different. A fresh world opens up with each new work of crime fiction we pick up.

So whether you are looking for new books whose characters resemble those in titles that you already enjoy or want to strike out in a new direction, these lists will help you. All of the titles here have character appeal as a strong part of their attraction for readers.

Dynamic Duos: Memorable Detective Teams

Since the days of Holmes and Watson, it is common for crime fiction to have at its center not a single detective but a pair of investigators (or sometimes a team). Teamwork and collaboration can be essential to the solution of the crime, and often one character's impetuousness is balanced by the reasoned approach of a partner. The detectives in this list all work as a pair to uncover the truth at the bottom of the puzzle.

Babson, Marian

Break a Leg, Darlings. **Trixie and Evangeline mysteries.** 1997. St. Martin's Press, ISBN 031215285X, 183p.

What are aging actresses to do? The plum roles are no longer coming in, and Trixie and Evangeline are out pounding the streets for work. Their search unwittingly puts them in danger when they unknowingly ask the wrong questions. As much a comedy of manners as a mystery, Trixie and Evangeline's adventures and arguments make them a wonderful pair.

Deaver, Jeffrey

The Bone Collector. **Lincoln Rhyme mysteries.** 1997. Viking, ISBN 067086871X, 432p.

In this book, Deaver introduced a wonderful, though unusual, pair of characters. Lincoln Rhyme is a brilliant forensic pathologist who is a quadriplegic. With Rhyme's extremely limited mobility, he has to rely on his partner, police officer Amelia Sachs, for the physical parts of the investigation. These are dark and violent stories. Here a serial killer is stalking New York, committing gruesome crimes. But it is as much the interaction between Rhyme and Sachs that makes for fascinating and suspense-filled reading.

George, Elizabeth

A Great Deliverance. **Thomas Lynley mysteries.** 1989. Bantam Books, ISBN 0553052446, 305p.

Often the sparks that two characters create when they are thrown together in a tense situation make for interesting reading. George pairs the aristocratic, charming Inspector Thomas Lynley with working-class Detective Sergeant Barbara Havers. Havers resents Lynley for his background but is forced to work with him on the case of a young girl who has apparently murdered her father with an axe. In order for the case to be solved, the two must come to a working relationship, and it is this process that gives the story much of its fascination.

Gerritsen, Tess
The Sinner. **Jane Rizzoli mysteries.** 2003. Ballantine Books, ISBN 0345458915, 352p.

A common pairing in crime fiction is for a police officer to work with a partner in one of the ancillary professions. In Gerritsen's Jane Rizzoli series, she pairs Rizzoli, a homicide detective, with medical examiner Maura Isles. With a team like this, Gerritsen can draw on the elements of both the police procedural and the forensic thriller. She does so to good effect in this tale of the murder of one nun and violent beating of a second in a Boston convent.

Hill, Reginald
⇨ *Bones and Silence*. **Dalziel and Pascoe mysteries.** 1991. Dell, ISBN 0440209358, 448p.

Hill takes the theme of the rough-edged junior officer and the more sophisticated superior officer and turns it on its head in the popular Dalziel and Pascoe mysteries. Superintendent Dalziel is outspoken, coarse, and boorish, whereas his junior partner, Inspector Pascoe, is mannered and introspective. Despite these differences, Pascoe and Dalziel manage to work well together, and the interplay between them adds to the appeal of the novels. Here, a somewhat inebriated Dalziel is witness to the death of a woman, but is it murder or suicide?

Hillerman, Tony
Skinwalkers. **Joe Leaphorn and Jim Chee mysteries.** 1990. HarperTorch, ISBN 0061000175, 320p.

The old pro detective in conflict with the brash young recruit is a common theme in crime fiction. Hillerman explores this territory in a novel fashion. Set in the Southwest, Hillerman's series features two tribal police officers. Joe Leaphorn, the elder of the two, is a longtime policeman, with faith in the traditional methods of policing. Jim Chee, though younger, is driven by the traditions of his Navajo roots. The blend of mysticism and mystery make for fascinating reading. Here, the pair faces three murders that may be linked to witchcraft.

Perry, Anne
The Cater Street Hangman. **Thomas and Charlotte Pitt mysteries.** 1979. St. Martin's Press, ISBN 031212385X, 247p.

What could make for a more interesting detecting pair than a husband-and-wife team? Even if in Victorian England it is not quite proper for the wife to be involving herself in something as unseemly as murder. Thomas Pitt is a police inspector from a working-class background, and Charlotte Ellison is from an aristocratic family. In the course of investigating the deaths of five young London women, Thomas and Charlotte cross paths, and they fall in love despite the difference in social status. Charlotte's social connections and her entrée into the houses of the wealthy make her an indispensable resource for Thomas throughout the series.

Zubro, Mark Richard

Drop Dead. **Paul Turner mysteries.** 1999. St. Martin's Minotaur, ISBN 0312205325, 256p.

Zubro breaks ground in the traditional detecting-pair realm by making one of his pair of Chicago detectives, Paul Turner, an openly gay father of two boys. Turner is partnered with Buck Fenwick, who is decidedly straight, and cynical to boot. The pleasure here comes from the naturalness with which Zubro portrays the interactions between Fenwick and Turner. These are two men who respect and like each other and are dedicated to getting the job done. In this case, solving the mystery of the death of a famous male model, who fell from the penthouse of a Chicago hotel.

"Hey Cisco, Hey Pancho": Sidekicks in Crime Fiction

We can't all be the Lone Ranger, and crime fiction has a host of not-quite-lead characters who still have a crucial role to play. The function of the sidekick in crime fiction varies, but it is never easy. Some, like Sherlock Holmes's Dr. Watson, serve as a foil to the intelligence of the investigator. They are there so that everyone knows how smart the detective really is. Others are the action figures doing the grunt work of the investigation and frequently taking the beatings and bullets that are really aimed at the main sleuth. Still others are there to provide backup muscle when needed. In all cases, though, the interaction between these faithful companions and the main character provides much of the pleasure to the reader. Here are some of crime fiction's memorable subordinates.

Burke, James Lee

Neon Rain. **Dave Robicheaux mysteries.** 2002. Pocket, ISBN 0743449207, 275p.

Burke's Louisiana-based mysteries are filled with dangerous, violent men, and Cletus Purcel is one of them. Fortunately, he is on the same side as investigator Dave Robicheaux, more or less. Purcel is exactly the sort of man you want to have watching your back, but he is also impetuous and prone to taking matters into his own hands. In *Neon Rain*, Robicheaux finds himself in deep trouble when he refuses to give up on an investigation that has links to the Mob, Latin American drug lords, and the Nicaraguan Contras. It's a good thing that Purcel has got his back.

Crais, Robert

L.A. Requiem. **Elvis Cole mysteries.** 1999. Doubleday, ISBN 0385495838, 382p.

Sometimes a sidekick moves out of the wings to take center stage for a book in a series. Elvis Cole is a wisecracking LA private detective who is frequently assisted in his jobs by a former LAPD officer, the honest, loyal, and reserved Joe Pike. Crais centers this story on Pike, who is falsely accused of murder, and on Elvis's attempts to clear his buddy. The story explores Pike's youth and early work on the LAPD, both of which offer clues to the current investigation.

Doyle, Arthur Conan
A Study in Scarlet. 2004. Wildside Press, ISBN 0809597411, 168p.

Dr. Watson is one of the most enduring and most long-suffering of sidekicks. Watson, of course, is the partner of the eminent consulting detective Sherlock Holmes. Throughout the course of the Holmes books, Watson puts up with much condescension from Holmes, about his understanding of Holmes's methods and his chronicles of Holmes's cases. But the good doctor is a true sidekick, loyal at all times, and like many other sidekicks he comes in for his share of buffets and blows. *A Study in Scarlet* introduces both Holmes and Watson to readers and to each other.

Mosley, Walter
***Black Betty*. Easy Rawlins mysteries.** 1994. W. W. Norton, ISBN 0393036448, 255p.

Raymond Alexander is an unstable and amazingly troubled man. Nicknamed "Mouse," Alexander is also the sometime friend of Mosley's hero, Easy Rawlins. There are times when Mouse is as likely to shoot Easy as to assist him, but he also has stepped in when needed to save Easy's life. *Black Betty* finds Easy searching for a missing housekeeper, and Mouse is out of jail and on the hunt for the man who sent him there. Mosley deftly captures the feel of LA in the early 1960s, and the interplay between Mouse and Easy is superb. Readers who want to further explore this relationship should try *Gone Fishin'* (Black Classic Press, 1997), which is a prequel to Mosley's Rawlins books that explores the roots of their uneasy friendship.

Parker, Robert B.
***Double Deuce*. Spenser mysteries.** 1992. Putnam, ISBN 0399137211, 242p.

Often, sidekicks are men of dubious reputation. A criminal background is usually not a concern and is frequently an asset, as it can give the detective access to the underworld when necessary. In Parker's Spenser novels, Hawk, a former Mob enforcer, is a frequent companion of Spenser. Hawk is cool, tough, and can be extremely scary when needed, all excellent assets in a sidekick. In *Double Deuce,* Hawk comes more to the forefront as he and Spenser battle drug gangs in Boston's Double Deuce projects.

Shelby, Jeff
***Wicked Break*. Noah Braddock mysteries.** 2006. Dutton, ISBN 0525949542, 246p.

The banter between the detective and the sidekick is one of the pleasures in these sorts of stories. Jeff Shelby's *Wicked Break* has that in great supply.

Noah Braddock and Carter Hamm are surfing buddies. There is nothing more fun for the two of them than to be out on the waves. But Noah is also an occasional PI, and when he needs muscle, the action-focused Carter is there to back him up. Here, the pair finds themselves caught up in an action-packed world of white supremacists, San Diego gangs, and guns.

Stout, Rex
⇨*Black Orchids*. **Nero Wolfe mysteries.** 1992. Crimeline, ISBN 0553257196, 208p.

A corpulent, sybaritic detective who generally refuses to leave his apartment is not going to be too successful without a sidekick. Fortunately for the orchid-loving Nero Wolfe, he has Archie Goodwin to do the hard work of investigation and to take the knocks as well. Goodwin is no lackey though, standing up to Wolfe when necessary. In this case, an orchid show lures Wolfe out of his home, and when a murder occurs at the show, Wolfe and Goodwin are called on to investigate.

Smarter than the Average Bear: Master Detectives

Then there are those geniuses of detection who really do not need any assistance from a partner or a sidekick. Oh, they may take advantage of having another body in for the bust if needed, but it is really their mastery of the art of sleuthing, and often their ego, that is on display in these mysteries. The talents vary: Some have astute powers of observation, some are skilled at making connections, others have vast knowledge of the criminal underworld, and still others can get people talking. In all cases, though, these are the detectives that you really do not want to be tracking you down; they are relentless, clever, and they always get their man. These detectives are less common in contemporary crime fiction, in which the wounded and all-too-human detective is increasingly typical.

Akunin, Boris
Death of Achilles. **Erast Fandorin mysteries.** 2006. Random House Trade Paperbacks, ISBN 0812968808, 336p.

Russian diplomat and investigator Erast Fandorin is back in Moscow after a sojourn in Japan. Fandorin is clever, witty, handsome, and observant. He is also more than ready to take on physical attacks, having been schooled in the martial arts while in the East. The death of a popular Russian general and the subsequent violence it precipitates require Fandorin to step in and locate the assassin.

Carr, John Dickson
Hag's Nook. **Gideon Fell mysteries.** 1985. International Polygonics, ISBN 0930330285, 190p.

If Sherlock Holmes is the father of the forensic school of crime solving, Gideon Fell, hero of John Dickson Carr's crime novels, is the forerunner of those detectives who think their way to the solution. The corpulent, beer-drinking historian never bends his knee for a clue, but he is a master at tying together seemingly unrelated clues. *Hag's Nook* is a classic locked-room mystery with a tinge of the supernatural.

Christie, Agatha
⇨ *The Mysterious Affair at Styles*. **Hercule Poirot mysteries.** 2002. Wildside Press, ISBN 1592248888, 188p.

The Mysterious Affair at Styles introduced readers to that master of ratiocination, Belgian detective Hercule Poirot. Poirot is a dandy, vain of his appearance, and supremely confident in his abilities, and it is rare that his "little grey cells" let him down. Poirot's first case involves the death of a wealthy woman whose children, servants, and new husband all may have had reason to kill her. Poirot is called in to the case by his future sidekick, Captain Hastings, who is a friend of the family.

Preston, Douglas, and Lincoln Child
The Book of the Dead. **Pendergast trilogy.** 2006. Warner Books, ISBN 0446576980, 464p.

FBI Special Agent Aloysius Pendergast is a modern-day Sherlock Holmes: energetic, scornful of dim police officers, icily intellectual, trained in the martial arts of the East, and essentially indestructible. He needs all of these traits to survive the hatred of his brother, Diogenes, for unlike Mycroft Holmes, Pendergast's brother is a monument of evil. From escaping a maximum security cell to a final confrontation in New York's Museum of Natural History, this book moves at a rocket pace.

Quill, Monica
Sine Qua Nun. **Sister Mary Teresa mysteries.** 1986. Vanguard Press, ISBN 0814909264, 182p.

Like Rex Stout's Nero Wolfe, Sister Mary Teresa does not leave her home base (in this case not a New York City brownstone but a Chicago convent). Fortunately, she has a pair of young assistants to do the investigating, leaving Sister Mary Teresa the time to reflect on the clues, reject the red herrings, and come to the truth of the matter. The death of a porn writer and the TV host who challenged him are the challenges for the good sister in this outing.

Sayers, Dorothy
The Nine Tailors. **Lord Peter Wimsey mysteries.** 1989. Harcourt Brace Jovanovich, ISBN 0151658978, 39p.

Suave, elegant, perceptive, athletic, musical, a bibliophile, and a wealthy aristocrat, Lord Peter Wimsey is truly a renaissance man. He has taken up the hobby of solving crimes, not as a dilettante but to truly see justice done. Wimsey is deeply affected by the processes of justice. This is one of his most interesting cases, involving stolen emeralds, false identities, and bell ringing. Wimsey combines the forensic skill of Holmes with the intellectual capacity of Poirot.

Stout, Rex

Fer-de-Lance. **Nero Wolfe mysteries.** 1997. Crimeline, ISBN 0553278193, 304p.

> Surrounded by his prize orchids and with a four-star chef on premises, Nero Wolfe sees no need to leave his luxurious brownstone in New York City, even for the most demanding of clients. Besides, with a crack team of assistants to bring him the threads of the investigation, all Wolfe has to do is weave them into a pattern. And he is a master weaver. Wolfe is a crime solver to the well heeled, taking on cases that have baffled the police. Here, Wolfe wrestles with a murder on the golf course that tests his detecting abilities.

Is That a Clue I See before Me?: Bumbling Sleuths

If you are tired of these paragons of intellect before whom no criminal stands a chance, try turning to the adventures of their exact opposites: the bumbling detectives. These are the folks who only recognize a clue when they stumble over it and who rely as much on luck and the kindness of strangers to solve crimes as on their little gray matter. They may be amateur detectives or police officials, but in all cases the detectives on this list solve the crime in a roundabout fashion, usually accompanied by a heavy dose of humor.

Akunin, Boris

Sister Pelagia and the White Bulldog. **Sister Pelagia mysteries.** 2007. Random House, ISBN 0812975138, 288p.

> Sometimes the detective only appears to be incompetent to the outside world. This perceived dim-wittedness can be a potent weapon in the investigator's arsenal. Sister Pelagia is an unremarkable Russian nun, whose plain appearance and somewhat bumbling style lead people to underestimate her abilities. But the bishop knows that she is a clever and canny observer of human nature, and so he sends Pelagia to look into a series of deaths on his grandmother's estate, including the poisoning of her prized bulldogs.

Brewer, Steve

Dirty Pool. **Bubba Mabry mysteries.** 2003. Worldwide Library, ISBN 0373264623, 272p.

> If you are not the brightest of detectives, you probably need to be able to take your lumps. That is certainly the case with Albuquerque PI Bubba Mabry, who solves cases with tenacity and a tendency to leap into situations rather than through elegant deductions. But the self-deprecating PI is an appealing character as he tries to track down a large ransom payment that went astray.

Brightwell, Emily

Mrs. Jeffries on the Trail. **Inspector and Mrs. Jeffries mysteries.** 1995. Berkley, ISBN 042514691X, 232p.

Usually it is the hired help that provides the comic relief in crime fiction. Domestic servants, coachmen, and so forth frequently are foils for the brilliance of the detective. Not so here, in which the bumbling Inspector Jeffries would never solve a crime if not for the canny assistance of his housekeeper, Mrs. Jeffries. Highly observant and willing to forgo the laurels, Mrs. Jeffries tracks down the murderer of a flower seller in this cozy historical set in the Victorian period.

Cockey, Tim

The Hearse You Came in On. **Hitchcock Sewell mysteries.** 2001. Hyperion, ISBN 0786889624, 416p.

Baltimore undertaker Hitchcock Sewell can handle all the aspects of death. From the casket to the grave, Sewell has things under control. But when he turns to investigating murder, he finds himself out of his depth. Fortunately, Sewell hooks up with a policewoman investigating the same killing. They make an appealing couple.

Evanovich, Janet

One for the Money. **Stephanie Plum mysteries.** 2003. St. Martin's Paperbacks, ISBN 0312990456, 352p.

Stephanie Plum has lost her job buying lingerie for a Trenton, New Jersey, department store, and to support herself she takes a job with her cousin Vinnie's bail bond business. Plum has never worked as a bounty hunter, but what she lacks in abilities, she makes up for in enthusiasm and effort. Much of the humor in the stories arises from watching Plum get herself into tight straits and then seeing how she manages to get out of them.

Hall, Parnell

Murder. **Stanley Hastings mysteries.** 1987. D. I. Fine, ISBN 1556110588, 256p.

Stanley Hastings would be a better PI if he was not afraid of getting hurt or into trouble. In this outing, it is only his sense of self-preservation that motivates him to take up the investigation of the murder of a pimp, who was blackmailing a friend of Stanley's wife. Found with the body while trying to recover a compromising video, Stanley must save himself from being charged by uncovering the real killer.

Pears, Iain

The Raphael Affair. **Jonathan Argyll and Flavia DiStefano mysteries.** 1998. Berkley, ISBN 0425166139, 240p.

Here, Pears introduces impoverished doctoral art student Jonathan Argyll, whose identification of a painting as a possible Raphael sets off a furor in the art world, especially when the painting is destroyed. But was it a real Raphael or not? It is up to the hapless Argyll to work with the staff of Rome's art theft and forgery squad to uncover the truth.

Strohmeyer, Sarah

⇨ *Bubbles Unbound*. **Bubbles Yablonsky mysteries.** 2002. Signet, ISBN 0451205448, 352p.

Bubbles Yablonsky enjoys the hairdressing trade in Lehigh, Pennsylvania, but in an effort to expand her horizons, she takes up reporting for the local paper. Her investigations lead her into a variety of perils, mostly as a result of her naïveté. Despite these tribulations, Bubble forges ahead in her pursuit of justice, assisted by a fascinating array of relatives and friends.

White Knights and Fixers: Solving Crimes and Righting Wrongs

The annals of crime fiction are full of fixers. Whether they are police officers, PIs, or amateurs, these are the investigators who step in when the law seems at a loss to bring justice to the world. Sometimes it is simply for the money, but often these are characters who willingly place themselves in jeopardy to create a society in which justice is accessible to all. They may not fight fairly, and they often skirt the letter of the law in upholding its spirit, but when you need them, it is good to know that the fixers are in.

Chesney, Marion

Snobbery with Violence. **Harry Cathcart mysteries.** 2004. St. Martin's Paperbacks, ISBN 0312997167, 256p.

There are indiscretions that the upper crust would prefer to keep hidden from the eyes of society and the law. Fortunately, misdemeanors that could be an embarrassment can be handled discretely and professionally by Harry Cathcart. Back from the Boer Wars, and as a second son of a titled family, Harry is in need of some of the ready. He uses his social connections and his wits to foil blackmailers, warn off inappropriate husbands, and uncover the solution to a murder.

Crais, Robert

Voodoo River. **Elvis Cole mysteries.** 1996. Hyperion, ISBN 0786889055, 416p.

Elvis Cole is an LA private investigator with a soft spot for those who are down on their luck. Here, he takes on an apparently straightforward case, tracking down the birth parents of a local TV personality. His journey into Cajun Louisiana takes him deeper into mystery than he expected, though, and when a death occurs, Cole decides that it is up to him to avenge that killing.

Haywood, Gar Anthony
Fear of the Dark. **Aaron Gunner mysteries.** 1990. Penguin, ISBN 0140131531, 192p.

   The fixers often can be found in communities that feel that the law is indifferent to their problems. The murder of two black men by a white man raises racial tensions in LA, especially when the sister of one of the victims feels that the police are turning a blind eye to the crime. She seeks out Aaron Gunner, who gave up PI work for more steady labor, and he agrees to take on the investigation. Gunner's strong social conscience marks the series.

MacDonald, John D.
Nightmare in Pink. **Travis McGee mysteries.** 1995. Fawcett, ISBN 0449224147, 304p.

   Travis McGee is a classic fixer. He takes on cases that seem hopeless and that put him into substantial danger, and usually he is as much motivated by a soft heart as by the fee. Here, McGee's friend, a wounded war vet, asks for help. The vet's sister has lost her fiancé in a mugging but thinks that there was more to his death. McGee takes on the investigation with his usual mix of wit and fists.

Mosley, Walter
⇨ *Devil in a Blue Dress*. **Easy Rawlins mysteries.** 1990. W. W. Norton, ISBN 0393028542, 219p.

   Mosley's Easy Rawlins is another fixer whose need to see justice done leads him to take on burdens that he would rather let go. Set in the African American community in 1940s LA, *Devil in a Blue Dress* finds Rawlins fired from his job and in need of work. He takes on a job for a local mobster, tracking down a missing white woman who has a bundle of cash. Rawlins moves back and forth in the white and black communities, and truth is his guide.

Paretsky, Sara
Indemnity Only. **V. I. Warshawski mysteries.** 1991. Dell, ISBN 0440210690, 336p.

   Most of the fixers that you will find in crime fiction are men, but the 1990s saw an increase in women taking on the white knight role. Sara Paretsky's V. I. Warshawski is one of the best. V. I. has a strong social conscience that leads her to take on corruption wherever she finds it. She also commits herself wholeheartedly to the pursuit of justice, regardless of the cost she will pay. In *Indemnity Only,* V. I. is hired to find a missing couple. The boy turns up dead, and V. I. finds herself warned off the case with a terrible beating. But she refuses to give in and finds herself facing corrupt unions, insurance fraud, and the Mob.

Parker, Robert B.
Mortal Stakes. **Spenser mysteries.** 1987. Dell, ISBN 0440157587, 336p.

   Like many fixers, Parker's Spenser lives by a strict code of personal standards. He will not shoot a man in ambush, and his code seems to require that he put himself in danger before responding violently. When Spenser begins to investigate why Boston Red Sox pitcher Marty Raab is losing games he should be winning, he discovers that blackmailers are holding Raab prey to his wife's past. Spenser steps in to set things right in his own inimitable fashion.

Wilson, F. Paul
All the Rage. **Repairman Jack mysteries.** 2001. Tor, ISBN 0812566548, 512p.

Repairman Jack is not going to come to fix your washer or dryer, but when things get tough and you need someone who will take on anyone, he's the man to call. Jack's concerns are with the fabric of the universe, but like the other fixers in this list, he operates with a moral code and a sense of justice. Repairman Jack is a fascinating study in violence and compassion, and the stories have an intriguing touch of the supernatural. Here, Jack tracks down those responsible for a new drug that causes people to act out their most violent impulses.

Dark Heroes: Sleuths on the Edge

Much contemporary crime fiction features detectives who have been wounded in some fashion, physically or psychologically. These novels are as much about the precarious state of the human condition as about the solution to a crime. Their protagonists are all the more human for their failings, though, and the stories provide readers with a realistic portrait of the struggle to lead a good life.

Bruen, Ken
The Guards. **Jack Taylor mysteries.** 2004. St. Martin's Minotaur, ISBN 0312320272, 304p.

Fired from the Irish national police force for excessive drinking and finally for punching a well-connected politician, Jack Taylor's life is breaking into pieces. He continues to drink heavily and takes on work as a finder, not as a PI. As he says, a private investigator is too close to an informer in Ireland. Taylor only gains a sense of redemption in his search for truth. Here, Taylor's investigation into the apparent suicide of a friend's daughter leads to more violence and betrayal.

Burke, James Lee
A Morning for Flamingos. **Dave Robicheaux mysteries.** 1991. Avon, ISBN 0380713608, 384p.

Dave Robicheaux is a former New Orleans cop, who has just rejoined the force. In addition to an alcohol problem, Robicheaux is haunted by the death of his wife, murdered in an earlier novel in the series. The struggle to live up to one's own moral code is at the heart of Burke's novels. The mood of the series is somber, but *A Morning for Flamingos* is particularly so, as Robicheaux goes back to New Orleans and must confront his past.

Kaminsky, Stuart
Retribution. **Lew Fonesca mysteries.** 2002. Forge, ISBN 0812540360, 256p.

Kaminsky's Lew Fonesca is one of the most damaged of investigators. The death of his wife has left Fonesca in the depths of depression, and he has left his native Chicago for Florida, where he works as a process server. In this entry, Fonseca is looking for two missing persons, a teenage girl and an elderly woman. Both investigations put Fonesca in danger, and this melancholy man makes his way as best he can toward justice.

Mankell, Henning
Faceless Killers. **Kurt Wallander mysteries.** 2003. Vintage, ISBN 1400031575, 288p.

In Mankell's first Kurt Wallander mystery, Swedish police officer Wallander's life is increasingly somber. His wife has left him, he is estranged from his daughter, and his elderly father's health is waning. Wallander turns to drink for solace but finds no comfort there. His life is further complicated when he is called on to investigate the brutal killing of an elderly farming couple, apparently by recent immigrants. A strong sense of Nordic dreariness pervades the book.

Parker, T. Jefferson
Storm Runners. 2007. William Morrow, ISBN 0060854235, 384p.

The heroes of Parker's stand-alone crime novels face inner demons as often as they face physical enemies. A bomb meant to kill San Diego policeman Matt Stromsoe leaves him terribly wounded physically but with even greater damage done to his psyche. Stromsoe's wife and son were killed in the blast, and the killer was caught. Nonetheless, Stromsoe's life is in ruins. He leaves the force and takes a job working personal security, but a series of incidents leads Stromsoe back to the man behind the killing of his wife and child.

Rankin, Ian
⇨ *Knots and Crosses*. **Inspector Rebus mysteries.** 1995. St. Martin's Paperbacks, ISBN 0312956738, 228p.

Scottish Police Inspector John Rebus is a dark man. He is divorced, alienated from his family, smokes and drinks to excess, and has few friends on the Edinburgh police force. It is the search for justice for the victims of horrific crimes that redeems him. Rebus's own dour mood is amply matched by Rankin's harsh depictions of the lives of the poor and working class in dim and dreary Edinburgh.

Wambaugh, Joseph
The Choirboys. 1987. Dell, ISBN 0440111889, 384p.

There are no heroes at all in this brooding look at the LAPD. The choirboys of the title are a group of LA police officers who meet after work to drink and share the burdens of contemporary policing. But their sessions descend into something darker, and a death at one of the "choir practices" has been covered up. As Wambaugh details the cynical, unhappy lives of these officers, he slowly reveals the details of the killing.

May the Force Be with You: The Best Police Procedurals

Most of us try to avoid run-ins with the police, and as a result, we really don't know what life is like on the other side of the badge and the gun. The best of the police procedurals give us an insight into the complicated and dangerous world of contemporary policing. It is a world where long periods of calm and sometimes boredom can evaporate in seconds into adrenaline-filled turmoil. Police officers put themselves in danger every day, and that potential for danger shapes the way they view the world. The titles on this list all capture the complexity of life on the beat.

Connelly, Michael
Black Ice. **Harry Bosch mysteries.** 2003. Warner Vision, ISBN 0446613444, 448p.

> Connelly's Harry Bosch novels are known for their relentlessly clear portrayal of life in the LAPD. Connelly has a firm command of the internal operations of the police and uses that knowledge to craft a believable and sobering tale. Bosch does not suffer fools gladly, an attitude that puts him at odds with his superiors on the force. Here, he continues to investigate the apparent suicide of a narcotics officer, despite insistence from above that he back off the case.

Constantine, K. C.
⇨ *Always a Body to Trade*. **Mario Balzic mysteries.** 2002. David Godine, ISBN 1567921914, 256p.

> Since 1972, Constantine has been chronicling the life and work of Mario Balzic, police chief in a dying Pennsylvania steel town. Constantine captures the ebb and flow of police work and is especially good at depicting the personal nature of policing in a small town. In this entry in the series, conflict arises when a federal narcotics team comes to town and deaths follow their trail.

Holton, Hugh
Chicago Blues. **Larry Cole mysteries.** 1997. Forge, ISBN 0812544641, 384p.

> The late Hugh Holton's day job as Chicago police detective lends an air of brutal realism to his novels featuring Chicago police Commander Larry Cole. Holton has a command of police procedures as well as an ear for the language of the force. Here, Cole investigates the murder of two mobsters, which may have been committed by a former cop, now serving as a bodyguard. Cole confronts the Chicago Mob and corrupt Chicago politics.

James, P. D.
A Taste for Death. **Adam Dalgliesh mysteries.** 1998. Ballantine, ISBN 0345430581, 480p.

With their appealing characters, compelling mysteries, and forensic details, James's novels featuring Scotland Yard Commander Adam Dalgliesh will appeal to a variety of readers. Readers interested in the details of police work will find much to enjoy here, as Dalgliesh and his team investigate the deaths of an indigent and a well-known politician. James shows the importance of the interaction between the officers to the success of the investigation.

Malone, Michael
Uncivil Seasons. **Hillston mysteries.** 2001. Sourcebooks, ISBN 1570717559, 355p.

Like K. C. Constantine, Malone excels at depicting the role of the police in a small community, in this case in the North Carolina Piedmont. Malone's police officers are very much part of the community they serve, a position that complicates matters when a series of deaths among the social elite need to be investigated. Malone's detectives come from the opposite ends of Hillston's social spectrum, and Malone puts this contrast to good use in the investigation.

Marric, J. J.
Gideon's Day. **George Gideon mysteries.** 1985. Madison Books, ISBN 0812881974, 304p.

Marric, a pseudonym for the amazingly prolific crime novelist John Creasey, defined the British police procedural in this initial entry in the George Gideon series. Over the course of a single day, multiple threads, some of which tie together, give readers a glimpse at the breadth of work undertaken by Scotland Yard. Superintendent Gideon and a cast of believable police officers and detectives make this older series a must read for fans of police procedurals.

McBain, Ed
Hail, Hail the Gang's All Here. **87th Precinct mysteries.** 2001. Warner Books, ISBN 0446609684, 224p.

J. J. Marric's equal in the United States is Ed McBain, known for his long-running series of novels about the patrol officers and detectives of the 87th Precinct. McBain presents the reader with an accurate portrayal of the sights, the smells, and the sounds of police work. The language and the police techniques always ring true. Here, multiple stories move from the routine to the chilling, each depicting an essential element of the lives and work of the members of the 87th Precinct.

Robinson, Peter
Final Account. **Inspector Banks mysteries.** 2004. Avon, ISBN 0060502169, 320p.

The tribulations of small-town policing are not limited to the United States, as Robinson demonstrates in his series set in Yorkshire, England.

Robinson frequently looks at the changes that have come to the community, as reflected in the crimes committed there. The interplay between Banks and the other members of the force is an essential part of the stories. Here, Banks teams up with a young woman constable to investigate a brutal murder.

The Force Is No Longer with You: Ex-Cops on Their Own

On the other end of the spectrum are those detectives who once were part of the thin blue line but no longer are on the force. Sometimes, they have retired, but more often there is some sort of conflict at the heart of the move to private detecting. These stories often feature contrasts: the camaraderie of working as part of the police force compared to the loneliness of the PI and the ability of the PI to work on the edges of legality versus the more stringent rules the police should follow. There also is the conflict that often arises between the private investigator and the police. The titles here feature the best of the ex-cops.

Bloom, Elizabeth
The Mortician's Daughter. 2006. Mysterious Press, ISBN 0892967862, 320p.
    Ginny Lavoie has been suspended from the NYPD for tampering with evidence and is at loose ends. So she heads back to her home town in Massachusetts, where she is called on to investigate the killing of a young man, the son of one of Lavoie's old friends. As in many ex-cop stories, the local police blend dishonesty and incompetence, and Lavoie's search for the killer puts her in danger from all sides.

Bruen, Ken
Priest. **Jack Taylor mysteries.** 2007. St. Martin's Minotaur, ISBN 0312341407, 304p.
    Alcohol was responsible for Jack Taylor's dismissal from the Irish Guard (the national police force). The loss of his job and his own continuing self-destructive behavior have spiraled increasingly out of control, and this latest book in the series finds Taylor virtually friendless and in a mental hospital. His only solace, outside the bottle, is in the search for justice in a bleak world. This is a dark series about loss and despair, but there are faint glimmers of redemption.

Castrique, Mark
A Dangerous Undertaking. **Barry Clayton mysteries.** 2006. Poisoned Pen Press, ISBN 1590582691, 254p.
    Barry Clayton's father is suffering from Alzheimer's disease and no longer able to run the family mortuary, so Clayton reluctantly gives up his job as a Charlotte, North Carolina, police officer to return home to the small town of

Gainesboro and take over the business. But a growing friendship with the local sheriff, Tommy Lee Wadkins, gives Clayton an outlet for his investigatory talents. When a young man bursts in on his grandmother's funeral, kills two mourners, and wounds Clayton, the pair investigate.

Craig, Philip

A Case of Vineyard Poison. **Jeff Jackson mysteries.** 1996. Avon, ISBN 0380726793, 224p.

Not all former policemen are haunted, troubled characters. Retired Boston PD Officer Jeff Jackson is enjoying life on Martha's Vineyard. The fishing is great, he has a lovely lady friend to whom he will soon be married, and he is contented with life. But when the body of a college student shows up on his driveway, and it turns out that she was poisoned, Jackson takes up the investigation. A more contemporary, cozy look at the life of an ex-cop.

Dunning, John

⇨*Booked to Die*. **Cliff Janeway mysteries.** 2000. Pocket Star, ISBN 0743410653, 432p.

Cliff Janeway is a successful Denver cop and an aficionado of rare books. When he is accused of brutality and suspended from the force, Janeway decides to quit and take up bookselling as a vocation. The ex-cop theme gives this series a darker edge than most bibliophile mysteries. Janeway's time on the force has left him with a somewhat cynical view of human nature. This first book in the series introduces Janeway, who investigates the brutal beating of a book scout.

Hillerman, Tony

The Shape Shifter. **Joe Leaphorn and Jim Chee mysteries.** 2006. Harper Collins, ISBN 0060563451, 288p.

Leaving the police force is a difficult transition to make, even when it is retirement and not dismissal. When Navajo police Lieutenant Joe Leaphorn retires, he finds time heavy on his hands. A letter from an old friend rekindles Leaphorn's interest in an unsolved crime from his early days on the force. When that friend dies in a suspicious accident, Leaphorn begins unraveling the threads of the old and new crimes.

McKevett, G. A.

Just Desserts. **Savannah Reid mysteries.** 1996. K Mass Paper, ISBN 1575660377, 320p.

When she refuses to give up on an investigation of a murder that might involve her boss, California police officer Savannah Reid is fired for exceeding the department's weight limits. Rather than suing, Reid sets up as a PI and begins her own investigation into the killing. Reid maintains a good relationship with her former police partner, Dirk Coulter, and this serves her well as she digs into murders and desserts in this fast-paced and humorous series.

Stansberry, Dominic
Chasing the Dragon. **Dante Mancuso mysteries.** 2006. St. Martin's Minotaur, ISBN 0312324685, 320p.

After leaving the San Francisco PD under a cloud, Dante Mancuso has gone to work for a security firm in New Orleans. When his father dies, Mancuso returns to San Francisco, ostensibly to attend the funeral but also to do a job for the firm, working with the feds to break up a drug ring. When Mancuso's uncle is killed, Mancuso comes under suspicion of the SFPD for the murder, and the interaction between the police and the former cop provides an interesting thread in the story.

They Also Serve: Nonpolice Officers

In addition to the police, there are a host of other criminal investigators who work for the government. Forest rangers, Fish and Wildlife officers, fire investigators, and others also find themselves probing into secrets and uncovering crime scenes. Frequently featuring interesting settings, these novels provide a new look at the procedural-focused crime story.

Barr, Nevada
⇨ *The Track of the Cat.* **Anna Pigeon mysteries.** 2003. Berkley, ISBN 0425190838, 272p.

Anna Pigeon has left New York City after the death of her husband and become a national park ranger in West Texas. Pigeon is dedicated, tough, and a bit cynical, and when a fellow ranger is killed, supposedly by a cougar, Pigeon is skeptical and investigates. She uncovers a host of tensions between rangers and locals as well as within the ranger community. The series has a strong environmental streak, and Barr writes beautifully about the landscape of the Southwest.

Box, C. J.
Open Season. **Joe Pickett mysteries.** 2002. Berkley, ISBN 042518546X, 304p.

Box's Joe Picket novels are set in the high country of Wyoming, where Pickett is a game warden. A man with a strong moral code, Pickett has a new job that becomes more complex when three bodies turn up, including a poacher Pickett had recently tried to arrest. Box has a feel for writing about the outdoors and understands the tensions faced by the game warden in an isolated rural community.

Heywood, Joseph
Running Dark. **Woods Cop mysteries.** 2005. Lyons Press, ISBN 1592286178, 304p.

In the 1970s, the environmental movement was just gaining steam and clashes between environmental officers and locals, who were used to hunting and fishing on government property, became common. Michigan conservation officer Grady Service finds himself caught up in this conflict on his first assignment in Michigan's Upper Peninsula (UP). Heywood's story is a great mix of forestry and characters.

Johansen, Iris
Firestorm. 2005. Bantam, ISBN 0553586491, 368p.

Fire investigation is a grueling job, and Kerry Murphy is known to be good at it, with the help of her dog, Sam. Only, as it turns out, Sam is just a figurehead for Murphy's uncanny ability to sense the cause of a fire. When a former government scientist who had been working on a weapons program involving fire goes rogue, the government wants to recruit Murphy to track him down. The book is a fast-paced thriller with some memorably frightening scenes of fire.

Russell, Kirk
Night Game. **John Marquez mysteries.** 2005. Chronicle Books, ISBN 0811850447, 368p.

John Marquez left the U.S. Drug Enforcement Administration for the ostensibly less dangerous world of the California Department of Fish and Game. In this second entry in the series, Marquez is heading up an investigation into the poaching of bears, whose parts are sold to the overseas market. The poachers are a violent bunch, and corrupt politicians, local ties, and murder complicate the investigation. Environmental issues and a strong sense of place mark the book as well.

Speart, Jessica
Unsafe Harbor. **Rachel Porter mysteries.** 2006. Avon, ISBN 0060559616, 288p.

Not all Fish and Wildlife officers work in the wilds of the U.S. West. The illegal trafficking in animals goes on throughout the entry ports of the United States. Rachel Porter's work with Fish and Wildlife brings her home to New York in this series entry. The death of a woman wearing a shawl made from an endangered species touches off an investigation that soon has Porter looking into her past. The series has strong environmental appeal and memorable characters.

Reading the Bones:
Forensic Sleuths

Detectives who work in professional fields ancillary to law enforcement continue to be popular. In particular, the late 1990s saw a boom in forensic mysteries. Science has become an essential part of the solving of crimes. Here, the sleuth is skilled at deciphering mysteries from the details of the crime scene and the body. The stories here range from the graphic to the more cerebral, but they all have at the center a strong focus on the crime scene details and their value to detection.

Bass, Jefferson
Carved in Bone. **Body Farm mysteries.** 2006. Harper, ISBN 0060759828, 352p.

Bill Bass, founder of the Body Farm and noted forensics innovator, is half of the pseudonymous writing team for this series. Set on the Body Farm, the story deftly mixes science and detection as the discovery of a mummified body in a Tennessee cave brings forensic anthropologist Bill Brockton (based on Bass) into the case. The book is filled with gooey forensic detail.

Beckett, Simon
The Chemistry of Death. 2006. Delacorte, ISBN 0385340044, 320p.

Following the death of his wife and daughter, forensic anthropologist David Hunter leaves detection and takes up practice as a village doctor. He is drawn back into forensics, though, when a neighbor is murdered, followed by a second killing. A mix of graphic forensic detail and an English setting, somewhat unusual for forensic crime fiction, makes this a winner.

Connor, Beverly
One Grave Too Many. **Diane Fallon mysteries.** 2003. Onyx, ISBN 0451411196, 400p.

Forensic work wears down many of its practitioners, and after years working for a human rights organization identifying remains from mass graves, Diane Fallon gives up forensic work to become a museum director. But it is hard to escape the past, and when an old friend, who is a police detective, asks her to identify some human bones, Diane is drawn back into the messy world of forensic detection.

Cornwell, Patricia
Body of Evidence. **Kay Scarpetta mysteries.** 2004. Pocket, ISBN 0743493915, 416p.

Cornwell is rightly credited with bringing forensic work to the forefront of crime fiction. With the debut of Virginia medical examiner Kay Scarpetta in *Postmortem,* Cornwell's attention to detail, especially gory detail, and understanding of the role of forensics in crime detection started the bones rolling. Here, Scarpetta undertakes a fast-paced investigation into the stabbing death of a Richmond, Virginia, writer.

Lovett, Sarah
⇨ *Dantes' Inferno*. **Dr. Sylvia Strange mysteries.** 2002. Pocket, ISBN 0671026461, 416p.

The interest in forensic detection has bifurcated, with one side providing graphic details of decapitated and otherwise mutilated bodies and the other branch moving in the more cerebral direction of forensic psychology. In these books, the killings may be equally awful, but the investigation explores the criminal psyche as much as fingerprints and knife directions. Dr. Strange is a frequent consultant into the criminal mind, and the details here are fascinating and creepy. Here, she becomes involved in the investigation of a museum bombing.

Reichs, Kathy
Deja Dead. **Temperance Brennan mysteries.** 2005. Pocket Star, ISBN 1416510559, 560p.

　　Reichs writes fast-paced, exciting novels with lots of forensic detail, drawing on her own background in forensic anthropology. Her lead, Temperance Brennan, is a Montreal-based forensic examiner, whose works takes her to a variety of locales. Here, Brennan investigates the murder of a woman that appears to be the work of a serial killer. There are enough graphic details here to satisfy the most jaded *CSI* fan.

Walker, Robert
Unnatural Instinct. **Jessica Coran mysteries.** 2003. Jove, ISBN 0515135291, 304p.

　　Part of the interest in forensic mysteries is the police procedural aspect, how the forensic specialist works with the law enforcement side of the investigation. Walker's Jessica Coran is a pathologist with the FBI, and these mysteries include ample medical and procedural details. This series entry finds Coran working with an FBI colleague to track down a kidnapped judge. A fast-paced mix of gruesome detail and thrilling detection.

The Game Is Still Afoot: Sherlock Holmes Continued

　　Readers of Arthur Conan Doyle's Sherlock Holmes mysteries know that Conan Doyle tried to end the series by having Holmes plunge to his death over Reichenbach Falls at the end of "The Final Problem." Holmes's popularity was so great, however, that reader demand forced Conan Doyle to resurrect Holmes in two more novels and three collections of stories. Since Conan Doyle's death, many more Sherlock Holmes books have been published. These range from traditional stories written in the Conan Doyle style to parodies of that style, and the stories take place in time from the Victorian period to the present day and even into the future. Most of these re-creations have Holmes and Watson as the main characters, but some authors have chosen minor characters from the original tales to be their protagonists. Irene Adler, the only woman to have ever bested Holmes; Edward Porter Jones, a former Baker Street Irregular; and even

Holmes's housekeeper, Mrs. Hudson, all have stories written about them. Here are some of the best of the Holmes continuations.

Carr, Caleb
The Italian Secretary. 2005. Little, Brown, ISBN 0316730831, 288p.

Noted for his historical fiction with a mysterious edge, Caleb Carr *(The Alienist)* takes up the mantle of Conan Doyle. With its suitably drear and oppressive Edinburgh setting and a puzzling mystery at the heart of the story, fans of Holmes and Watson will enjoy watching them in action again. Who killed the men in Holyrood Palace? Scottish nationalists? German assassins? Ghosts? *The Italian Secretary* is a suitably dark and exciting tale for Holmes enthusiasts.

Douglas, Carole Nelson
Good Night, Mr. Holmes. **Irene Adler adventures.** 1990. T. Doherty Associates, ISBN 0312932103, 408p.

To Holmes, she would always be "the woman." Actress Irene Adler is the only woman to have bested Sherlock Holmes (see Conan Doyle's "A Scandal in Bohemia"). Holmes and Dr. Watson appear as supporting characters in Douglas's books. The main character is Irene Adler, singer, actress, and adventurer. In between performances, Adler takes on cases, using much the same techniques of observation and deduction as Holmes. Douglas succeeds in replicating the atmosphere of Victorian England as well as introducing several well-known historical characters to the stories.

Fawcett, Quinn
The Flying Scotsman. **Mycroft Holmes mysteries.** 1999. Forge, ISBN 0312863640, 320p.

In the Conan Doyle stories, Mycroft Holmes bears a certain resemblance to a spider, sitting at the center of a web and interpreting the twitching of the strings. He is a shadowy figure, who at times "is the British Government." Fawcett brings Mycroft center stage in his re-creations. The stories have a political focus and the capture the feel of the originals.

Hockensmith, Steve
Holmes on the Range. **Holmes on the Range mysteries.** 2006. St. Martin's Minotaur, ISBN 0312347804, 304p.

Holmes and Watson appear here only as characters in the papers, but they are the heart and soul of the tale. It is the 1890s, and the Amlinger brothers are riding the range, herding cattle in Montana. Having been entertaining themselves with stories of Holmes and Watson from *Harper's Weekly,* the discovery of a dead cowhand gives the brothers a chance to do some "deducifyin'" in the style of their heroes. *Holmes on the Range* is a delightful homage to the originals and a fine story in its own right.

Hosier, Sidney
Elementary, Mrs. Hudson. **Emma Hudson mysteries.** 1996. Avon Books, ISBN
0380781751, 206p.

You cannot be landlady and housekeeper to Sherlock Holmes without
acquiring some detecting skills. At least that is what Mrs. Emma Hudson
has found from her observations of the master's technique. These skills
prove useful when Mrs. Hudson receives a telegraph from an old friend
asking her to send Sherlock Holmes to investigate a suspicious death. As
Holmes is unavailable, Mrs. Hudson goes herself. With the help of her
friend, Violet Warner, Mrs. Hudson investigates and solves the mystery of
Hadley Hall.

King, Laurie R.
⇨ *The Beekeeper's Apprentice*. **Mary Russell and Sherlock Holmes mysteries.** 1994. St. Martin's Press, ISBN 0312104235, 368p.

Retired to a life of beekeeping in Sussex, Sherlock Holmes is drawn back
into detecting by his encounter with an orphan, Mary Russell, who is as keen
an observer as he is. Their friendship blossoms, and, despite a significant age
difference, Russell and Holmes fall in love and marry. King does an excellent
job of presenting an older Holmes, and Mary Russell is an engaging character.
King clearly knows the original Holmes stories as well as other detective fiction set in the early twentieth century. These books are among the best of the
Holmes re-creations.

Meyer, Nicholas
The Canary Trainer. 1995. W. W. Norton, ISBN 0393312410, 224p.

Many Holmes continuations purport to be discoveries of lost manuscripts
of Dr. Watson, from that battered metal case of his. Meyer uses this conceit to
great success in his Holmes stories. This one is a tale from the lost years, after
Holmes's supposed death at Reichenbach. Holmes is playing violin in the Paris
Opera and must take on a ghost that is terrorizing singers and musicians alike.
Holmes meets the Phantom of the Opera. Meyer skillfully re-creates the world
of Holmes and Watson.

Trow, J. M.
The Adventures of Inspector Lestrade. **Sholto Lestrade mysteries.** 1998. First
World Publication Regnery Publishing, ISBN 0895263432, 224p.

In the original Holmes stories, Inspector Lestrade was presented as a bumbling police officer, more intent on making an arrest than on discovering the
truth. But J. M. Trow resurrects Lestrade's reputation in this delightful series.
In Trow's telling, it is Lestrade who has the brains and Holmes who is the
bungling detective. Appearances from historical characters add to the period
feel of the stories, and Trow concocts a clever puzzle and tells the story with a
mixture of humor and realism.

They Were Detectives, Too?:
Historical Characters as Detectives

Although there are many readers who apparently think that Sherlock Holmes and Dr. Watson were real, alas that is not the case. Fortunately, there are plenty of mysteries out there that do feature historical characters as the detective. Some of these take a very lighthearted approach, whereas others try to stick close to the historical facts. Readers who enjoy an interesting blend of history and detection should find some intriguing titles on this list. Stories here range from the sixteenth to the twentieth century and go back and forth across the Atlantic.

Barron, Stephanie
Jane and the Unpleasantness at Scargrave Manor. **Jane Austen mysteries.** 1996. Bantam, ISBN 055310196X, 289p.

> The discovery of several boxes of dust-covered family papers sets the stage for Barron's Jane Austen mystery series. Barron uses a formal style (including footnotes) that captures the feel of a Jane Austen novel and does a good job of creating a puzzling mystery. In this first entry, Jane is visiting a friend whose husband suddenly dies. Jane steps in to clear the widow of charges of murder.

Baxt, George
The Greta Garbo Murder Case. **Celebrity mysteries.** 1992. St. Martin's Press, ISBN 031206988X, 197p.

> Baxt is known for his series of mysteries featuring famous Hollywood stars of the early days of film and other celebrity detectives. If you are wondering how Dorothy Parker, Alfred Hitchcock, Mae West, or Humphrey Bogart might have approached detection, Baxt is your man. These are gossipy tales, with lots of name-dropping and cameos by celebrities. They make for fun reading for their peeks into the lives of the stars. Here, Greta Garbo investigates a series of murders with Nazi and espionage overtones.

Goulart, Ron
Groucho Marx, Private Eye. **Groucho Marx mysteries.** 1999. St. Martin's Press, ISBN 0312198957, 263p.

> For those readers looking for even more Hollywood glitter, Ron Goulart's Groucho Marx series is just the thing. It's the 1930s, and Groucho is starring in a new show as a fictional detective. When the mother of his supporting actress is arrested for offing a Hollywood MD, Groucho and his scriptwriter, Frank Denby, a former crime journalist, try to clear her name and track down the real killer. Denby narrates the stories, which are replete with Marxist humor (Groucho, not Karl) and Hollywood tidbits.

Hall, Robert Lee
London Blood. **Benjamin Franklin mysteries.** 1997. St. Martin's Press, ISBN
0312169086, 245p.

Hall's series takes for its main character Founding Father Benjamin Franklin. Set in London in the period prior to the Revolution, Franklin is assisted in his cases by his illegitimate son, Nicholas Handy, ostensibly the great-great-great-great-great-great-grandfather of Robert Lee Hall. Franklin is in London as the colonies' representative. Franklin was known for his curiosity, and he makes an able detective. Here, the killings of two girls leads Franklin and Handy to a debauched gentleman's club.

Harper, Karen
⇨ *Poyson Garden.* **Elizabeth I mysteries.** 1999. Delacorte Press, ISBN
0385332831, 320p.

As if she was not busy enough ruling England, according to Harper, Queen Elizabeth I also took the time to solve mysteries. Of course, given that from a young age she was faced with the possibility of her own demise at the hands of conspirators, this is no real surprise. Harper conjures up a believable English Court and has created some great supporting characters. In the first title in the series, Elizabeth is not yet queen, and she must investigate a series of deaths in her family that seem aimed at reducing her chances of succeeding to the throne.

Heck, Peter
Death on the Mississippi. **Mark Twain mysteries.** 1995. Berkley Prime Crime,
ISBN 0425149382, 290p.

The world of nineteenth-century riverboats is brought to life in this series featuring Mark Twain as the detective. Twain sets out from New York to give a series of lectures as a way of raising funds (and tracking down some buried gold along the Mississippi). Twain and his traveling secretary join forces to solve the death of a friend from Twain's days on the river. Heck offers the reader a historically authentic portrait of life on the Mississippi.

Palmer, William
The Detective and Mr. Dickens. **Charles Dickens mysteries.** 1990. St. Martin's
Press, ISBN 0312050739, 290p.

Writers Wilkie Collins and Charles Dickens team up here to take on a series of sexually driven murders. Ostensibly taken from Collins's journals, the pair joins Inspector William Field of the Metropolitan Protectives of London to solve the murders. The ambience of Victorian London is well reproduced from highlife to the seamy underbelly of Victorian mores.

Roosevelt, Elliott
Murder at Midnight. **Eleanor Roosevelt mysteries.** 1997. St. Martin's Press,
ISBN 0312965540, 240p.

During the 1930s and 1940s, the White House was a hotbed of murder and conspiracy, at least as described by Roosevelt in these well-crafted mysteries.

Roosevelt places his mother, Eleanor, at the heart of the stories, and it is her pursuit of justice for everyone that drives the investigations. In this entry, a member of President Roosevelt's brain trust is found dead at the White House, and a maid is accused. Eleanor believes her innocent, though, and sets out to find the real killer.

"Vengeance Is Mine," Saith the Lord: Religious Crime Solvers

The seal of the confessional prevents Catholic priests from revealing what is told to them during the sacrament of confession; however, there is no ban on members of the clergy acting as detectives. That's a great thing for mystery fans, as some of the most memorable detectives in crime fiction are priests, rabbis, monks, and nuns. The religious deal with good and evil in their day-to-day work. They understand the darkness the human heart holds and are rarely surprised by what they discover. They also have a sense of the possibility of redemption that blends with a demand for justice that is typical of mystery fiction.

Blake, Michelle

Earth Has No Sorrow. **Lily Connor mysteries.** 2001. G. P. Putnam, ISBN 0399147470, 257p.

Lily Connor is an Episcopalian priest who struggles with her faith and her relationships. She is not attached to a particular parish but rather serves the Boston Diocese by filling in where she is needed. Blake's books utilize the mystery to explore difficult questions of faith and belief. Here, an ecumenical Holocaust memorial service that Connor helped plan is vandalized and a good friend disappears. Connor's search for her friend uncovers some dark forces at work in Boston's churches.

Chesterton, G. K.

⇨ *Father Brown Omnibus*. 1983. Dodd, Mead, ISBN 0396081592, 993p.

The simple-seeming, unassuming English Catholic priest, Father Brown, never seeks out trouble. But he frequently seems to be on the scene when trouble strikes. These stories are deeply imbued with Chesterton's own deeply held Catholic faith. Father Brown does not look for clues à la Sherlock Holmes. Rather, he looks into the hearts of people, and his understanding of the human heart leads him to the solution of the crime. "The Blue Cross" is an excellent place to start. Father Brown matches wits with the famed jewel thief Flambeau.

Kemelman, Harry
The Friday the Rabbi Slept Late. **Rabbi David Small mysteries.** 2002. I Books, ISBN 0743434870, 208p.

Like G. K. Chesterton's Father Brown, Rabbi David Small does not rely on forensic evidence to solve mysteries. Rather, it is his understanding of the Talmud and Talmudic thinking that enable him to tease out the thread of truth from a tangled skein of possibilities. Rabbi Small heads a synagogue in Connecticut, and his friendship with the police chief of the community offers him the opportunity to assist in bringing justice to the world. The rabbi is motivated by the search for justice, tempered by mercy.

McInerny, Ralph
Triple Pursuit. **Father Dowling mysteries.** 2001. St. Martin's Press, ISBN 031226948X, 384p.

Set in the Catholic parish of Saint Hillary's, presided over by the thoughtful and observant Father Roger Dowling, these stories are valued as much for the characters and their spiritual sense as for the mystery. Father Dowling's close friendship with police Captain Phil Keegan results in the priest's involvement in crimes that feature parishioners of Saint Hilary's. In this case, three deaths that seem to be unrelated are tied together with Father Dowling's assistance. This is a fine mystery series with cozy overtones.

Peters, Ellis
A Morbid Taste for Bones. **Brother Cadfael mysteries.** 1994. Time Warner (reprint), ISBN 0751517496, 256p.

The stories in Ellis Peters's Brother Cadfael series follow the rhythms of monastic life in the Benedictine abbey at Shrewsbury. Cadfael, a former crusader who came to the monastery late in life, uses his experiences and his native wisdom to unravel crimes, often with the assistance of Hugh Berringer, sheriff of Shrewsbury. The stories present a fascinating look at life in a medieval abbey and are graced with a host of interesting characters. Here, the brothers of Shrewsbury are on a trip to bring back the relics of a Welsh saint to lie at the abbey. They are opposed by the villagers where the saint reposes, and when the leader of the opposition is killed, Cadfael's investigations bring the trip to a successful conclusion for all.

Thurlo, Aimee, and David Thurlo
Bad Faith. **Sister Agatha mysteries.** 2002. St. Martin's Press, ISBN 0312290810, 290p.

The last place one might look for a detective would be in a cloistered monastery in New Mexico. But when the monastery's chaplain is poisoned while celebrating Mass, it is fortunate that the order has Sister Agatha on hand to investigate. Her role as an extern means that Sister Agatha deals with the order's business in the outside world. Her contacts there and her understanding of her fellow religious lead her to the solution of the crime. The Thurlos' books present a contrast between the cloistered life inside the monastery and life outside its walls.

Tremayne, Peter
Absolution by Murder. **Sister Fidelma mysteries.** 1996. St. Martin's Press, ISBN 0312139187, 274p.

> Set in seventh-century Ireland, the Sister Fidelma series centers around the crime-solving abilities of an Irish nun, Sister Fidelma, and a Saxon monk, Brother Eadulf. Fidelma is not only a religious but also sister to the king of Munster and a skilled lawyer in courts of Ireland. Much of the mystery in the series is rooted in the struggle for power between the old Celtic church and the newer church centered in Rome. In this title, the death of a powerful Irish abbess brings together Fidelma and Eadulf to investigate.

Woodworth, Deborah
Death of a Winter Shaker. **Sister Rose Callahan mysteries.** 1997. Avon, ISBN 038079201X, 213p.

> Even among the pacifist Shaker communities, murder sometimes stalks. The "winter Shaker" of the title is a person who pretends to Shaker beliefs in order to be taken in, fed, and housed by the community over the winter. When one such person comes to the North Homage Shaker community, he is taken in, but when he is found dead, it is the job of Sister Rose Callahan, an elder in the community, to determine if the crime was committed by an outsider or by a member of the community. Woodworth provides ample detail about the little-known life in a Shaker community, and Sister Rose is an appealing detective.

Family Ties: Home Life and the Detective

Although there are many instances of crime fiction in which the detective is a loner, separated from society either intentionally or not, there are a growing number of stories in which family connections play an important role. These family ties may be a direct part of the mystery, allowing the detective to more efficiently solve the crime, but other times the family story serves to humanize the detective, placing him or her in a context that is familiar to readers and offering a contrast to the violent and dark world of crime. This list presents some of the best husbands and wives and mothers and fathers in crime fiction.

Fusilli, Jim
Closing Time. **Terry Orr mysteries.** 2002. Berkley, ISBN 0425187128, 320p.

> Terry Orr lost his wife and infant son to a killer, and he is left to care for his teenage daughter. His life becomes focused on tracking down the killer,

and he acquires a PI license to do so. But other cases come along, and Orr takes them on to support his hunt. Much of the pleasure in the story comes from the way Fusilli captures the tender relationship between Orr and his daughter. With a noir feel, great characters, and a real sense of Manhattan, Fusilli's book succeeds on many levels.

Leon, Donna

⇨ *Through a Glass Darkly*. **Guido Brunetti mysteries.** 2006. Atlantic Monthly Press, ISBN 0871139375, 272p.

The stories of two families are contrasted here in Leon's lovely prose. Her longtime hero is Italian police Commissario Guido Brunetti. Here, the commissario is drawn into the investigation of threats made by a wealthy glass-factory owner against his environmentalist son-in-law. The unhappiness of that family is underscored by the loving nature of Brunetti's relationships with his own wife and children.

Lewin, Michael

Family Planning. 1999. St. Martin's Press, ISBN 031224391X, 272p.

The lines between business and kin are blurred in the Lunghi clan living in Bath, England. Three generations of Lunghis participate in the family detective agency, though the crimes they are called on to solve are sometimes less important than the doings of the various members of the family. From the elderly grandparents to the newest generation, the Lunghis take on misdeeds both trivial and serious in this lighthearted look at English crime solving.

Maron, Margaret

Up Jumps the Devil. **Deborah Knott mysteries.** 1996. Warner Books, ISBN 0446604062, 304p.

Land and family are a potent mix, and one that can sometimes result in hurt feelings or worse. Serving in the North Carolina Piedmont, Judge Deborah Knott finds herself in the middle of a tangled web of family alliances and murder when an old friend is killed just after he refuses to sell family land to a developer. Judge Knott's relations to the family of the dead man are complicated by the fact that she was briefly married to his ne'er-do-well cousin. Maron depicts the intricate and twisting relational ties that are common in the South.

Muller, Marcia

Dead Midnight. **Sharon McCone mysteries.** 2002. Mysterious Press, ISBN 089296765X, 320p.

Sometimes, the family events in crime fiction parallel the mystery plot rather than contrast it. In this recent entry in Muller's Sharon McCone series, the detective is still suffering the effects of the suicide of her own brother. Called on to investigate the suicide of a young man who worked at an online magazine, her digging uncovers shady business practices and financial malfeasance at high levels as well as disturbingly unpleasant office politics. The effect of suicide on the survivors and the seamy side of the business world are equally featured here.

O'Hehir, Diane
Murder Never Forgets. **Carla Day mysteries.** 2005. Berkley Hardcover, ISBN 0425205851, 304p.

O'Hehir's story combines a compelling mystery with a look at the challenges that aging bring to both parents and children. Carla Day's father is suffering from Alzheimer's disease and lives in an assisted-living facility. Her father comes back from a walk with a story of seeing a woman being murdered, and no one is sure of the truth of the matter. When other odd things start happening at the home, Carla takes a job as an orderly to investigate and to keep an eye on her father, who is deteriorating. O'Hehir presents a moving portrait of a father and daughter.

Perry, Anne
The Hyde Park Headsman. **Thomas and Charlotte Pitt mysteries.** 1995. Fawcett, ISBN 0449223507, 352p.

In Victorian England, the social order was defined by class, and when Thomas Pitt, a police inspector from a working-class background, marries Charlotte Ellison, who is from an aristocratic family, her family is not too happy. Fortunately, the Pitts' marriage thrives, and Charlotte's social and family connections prove useful to Thomas in his work. Here, Charlotte and her sister are able to uncover a secret that allows Thomas to solve a series of beheadings.

Peters, Elizabeth
The Last Camel Died at Noon. **Amelia Peabody mysteries.** 1992. Warner Books, ISBN 0446363383, 448p.

Intrepid archaeologist Amelia Peabody is fortunate to have married an equally stalwart Egyptologist, Radcliffe Emerson. The developing relationship between the two is one of the pleasures of Peters's mysteries. Early in the series, the pair were blessed with a son, Ramses, whose growth from novel to novel adds to the family focus. Here, Peabody and Emerson and a teenaged Ramses set out on an expedition to locate an English archaeologist who has been lost in the Sudan.

Women of a Certain Age: And the Crimes They Solve

It might be almost a cliché: the older woman, usually single, who solves crimes in her community. She usually comes equipped with powers of observation that border on the nosy, an independent streak, and a community where people seem to be dropping like flies. These stories generally fall in the cozy category, in which the violence is limited and the murder takes place offstage, and they usually feature an equal blend of humor and mystery. Agatha Christie's Miss Marple is the paradigm of this sort of detective, and ever since *The Murder at the Vicarage,* readers have flocked to these stories. Here are some of the most interesting detectives of a certain age.

Atherton, Nancy
Aunt Dimity Digs In. **Aunt Dimity mysteries.** 1999. Penguin, ISBN 014027569X, 288p.

As proof of the undying popularity of older female detectives, Atherton's Aunt Dimity is not just of a certain age, she is dead. Her blue notebooks, though, allow Aunt Dimity to communicate with her corporeal companion, Lori Shepherd. Despite her mortal condition, Aunt Dimity meets all the criteria for the list. Here, Lori finds Aunt Dimity's advice helpful in unraveling a theft relating to an archaeological find in an English village.

Beaton, M. C.
⇨ *Agatha Raisin and the Quiche of Death.* **Agatha Raisin mysteries.** 1993. Fawcett, ISBN 0804111634, 192p.

The older woman sleuth seems to thrive in a country setting, where she can keep up with what is going on in the neighborhood. When Agatha Raisin moves from London to a Cotswold village, she tries to smooth her entry into the community by entering a baking contest. Unfortunately, her quiche poisons the judge, and Agatha has to use her wits to uncover the murderer. The series features a delightful cast of characters, including Agatha, who is a mix of irascibility and cleverness.

Carr, Josephine
My Very Own Murder. 2005. NAL Trade, ISBN 0451216466, 272p.

Anne Johnson is not your usual middle-aged sleuth. A well-off divorcee with two children and a Washington, DC, apartment, she is at least as interested in sex as she is in mysteries and almost as interested in drinking as in sex. But when a voice in her head tells her that a murder will be committed in the apartment complex in the next 30 days, Anne takes it on herself to discover the would-be killer and prevent the murder. Lots of humor and quirky characters make this a fun and fast read.

Douglas, Laramee
A Death in Dulcinea. 2005. Alligator Tree Press, ISBN 0971343020, 233p.

What could be better than one woman of a certain age? Laramee Douglas gives us three stalwart sleuths in *A Death in Dulcinea:* retired librarian Darby Matheson and her friends Wilhelmina and Ariana. The three are at the center of Dulcinea, Texas's, social world, so when a murder occurs at a benefit event and one of Darby's former students is accused, the three band together to prove his innocence.

Hammond, Gerald

On the Warpath. 2006. Severn House Publishers, ISBN 0727863669, 192p.

Not all elderly detectives are sweet old ladies. Helen Mercier served with the French Resistance in World War II, and she went on to be a successful journalist. Now in her eighties and enjoying the quiet life in England, Helen must brush off her undercover skills when her grandson is conned and robbed. She heads off to her old stomping grounds in Europe to help him recover his property.

Hart, Carolyn

Death on the River Walk. **Henrie O mysteries.** 2000. Avon, ISBN 038079005X, 336p.

Henrietta O'Dwyer Collins, Henrie O to her friends, is a somewhat more acerbic Miss Marple, but without the village base. A retired journalist and widow, Henrie O is an accomplished traveler, and mysteries seem to turn up wherever she goes. She uses a mix of charm and logic to solve crimes. Underneath a tough exterior is a compassionate heart that compels her to help those in need. In this installment in the series, Henrie O gets a call from an old friend whose granddaughter has disappeared in San Antonio. A mix of interesting characters, tight plotting, and local color make this a fascinating story.

Riggs, Cynthia

Paperwhite Narcissus. **Victoria Trumbull mysteries.** 2005. St. Martin's Minotaur, ISBN 0312339836, 256p.

Other than the dear departed Aunty Dimity, Victoria Trumbull wins the prize for the oldest of our sleuths. At 92, Victoria serves as a deputy police officer in the town of West Tilbury on Martha's Vineyard and knows everyone in town. When she loses her job writing for a local paper and is hired by a rival, she becomes involved in a competition between the two papers. Then, when a body washes ashore and one of the papers begins receiving obituary notices for people who then turn up dead, Victoria has to step in to track down the killer.

Feisty Females: Tough Women Detectives

Not all female detectives fit the neighborhood snoop model. There are an increasing number of women on the detecting scene who do not shy away from a fight and who use muscle as well as intellect to solve the mystery. Whether they are PIs, police officers, or amateur investigators, the women on this list can mix it up with the best of them.

Arruda, Suzanne
Mark of the Lion. **Jade del Cameron mysteries.** 2006. New American Library, ISBN 0451217489, 352p.

Jade del Cameron can handle wounded men, guns, and cars, skills that came in handy on the battlefields of France during the first World War. As an ambulance driver, Jade heard the dying requests of many soldiers. But when a request comes from the man who recently proposed to her, she has to follow up. The pilot's last words asked Jade to locate his missing brother, who disappeared in Africa, and following the armistice, Jade heads to the African jungle and into danger.

Bowen, Rhys
Murphy's Law. **Molly Murphy mysteries.** 2002. St. Martin's Minotaur, ISBN 0312984979, 256p.

When she accidentally kills the landowner's son who was trying to rape her, Molly Murphy is forced to flee from her family's home on an Irish estate. Amply equipped with courage and wits, she manages to join the Irish exodus to the United States, but while on the boat she has a run-in with one of her fellow émigrés. When he turns up dead on Ellis Island, Molly is suspect, and she heads into the grim streets of New York City's Irish slums to track down the real killer.

Clemens, Judy
Till the Cows Come Home. **Stella Crown mysteries.** 2004. Poisoned Pen Press, ISBN 1590580826, 265p.

Farming is not an easy life, and Stella Crown knows firsthand the physical strains that come with running a small dairy farm. A series of mishaps that puts her farm in jeopardy seems initially to be just a run of bad luck. But when a mysterious illness begins to affect other members of the farming community, Stella gets on her Harley and begins to investigate. A spirited, tough, but compassionate woman, Stella is a strong addition to the detecting community.

Colt, Jennifer
The Mangler of Malibu Canyon. **McAfee Twins mystery.** 2006. Broadway, ISBN 0767920120, 384p.

Colt's series features a pair of Harley-riding twin sisters, Kerry and Terry McAfee, who are prone to action and able to handle themselves in a fight. A fun mix of mystery, adventure, and humor, this entry in the series finds the twins trying to clear their great-aunt and a cousin from murder charges. The breezy California setting offers a host of great secondary characters as well as this pair of tough ladies.

Evanovich, Janet
One for the Money. **Stephanie Plum mysteries.** 2003. St. Martin's Paperbacks, ISBN 0312990456, 352p.

Evanovich deftly mixes humor, romance, and crime in her Stephanie Plum series. Plum is a bounty hunter, whose enthusiasm sometimes outpaces her abilities. But she is tough, smart-mouthed, and likable, and the series features a cast of other fascinating characters. The action is fast paced in this first title in the series as Plum makes her initial foray into tracking down a bail jumper.

Grafton, Sue

⇨ *A Is for Alibi*. **Kinsey Millhone mysteries.** 2005. St. Martin's Paperbacks, ISBN 0312938993, 320p.

Grafton was one of the earliest crime fiction writers to tap the tough female detective market. Kinsey Millhone has been the model for a host of other feisty women investigators. Raised by her aunt, who taught young Kinsey how to shoot, Millhone is a strong, thoughtful woman who runs a PI business in California. Unlike many of her later confederates, Millhone operates on her own much of the time, and the first-person narration gives the reader an interesting insight into her life. Here, she investigates an old murder in which the real killer seems to have gotten away with the crime.

Paretsky, Sara

Killing Orders. **V. I. Warshawski mysteries.** 2005. Signet, ISBN 0451214978, 368p.

Paretsky's series is probably the darkest in this list, both in tone and in level of violence. Set in Chicago, the series features a highly ethical PI, V. I. Warshawski. Unfortunately, her principles often take V. I. into dangerous territory, and she receives more then her share of physical violence. But she refuses to compromise her ideals, and her ability to fight and handle a gun stand her in good stead. Here, forged stock certificates lead V. I. to the dark side of Catholic Church politics and the Chicago Mafia.

Seranella, Barbara

No Man Standing. **Munch Mancini mysteries.** 2003. Pocket, ISBN 0743420330, 368p.

Munch Mancini has led a difficult life, overcoming heroin addiction, being prostituted by her father, arrests, and an assortment of other challenges. She is trying to go straight and is working as a mechanic and limo driver but is not able to completely shed her connections to the underbelly of 1970s Los Angeles. Seranella manages to make Munch an appealing character in spite of her questionable background, and her hard life makes the investigative work she takes on seem light by comparison. In this entry, Munch helps an old friend from her biker days whose parents have been murdered.

Toughest Guys: Two-Fisted Male Sleuths

Of course, male detectives can be just as tough and prone to violence as their female counterparts. The characters in the stories on this list all use their muscle as much as their brains in solving mysteries. Sometimes, they combine the two, but in a pinch, two fists or high-velocity firepower are what these tough guys turn to. Like the ladies on the previous list, these characters also take their share of beatings but accept that as part of the responsibility that comes with the job. These men often work in the gray area between right and wrong, and sometimes it is hard to really distinguish them from their antagonists.

Barre, Richard
Bearing Secrets. **Wil Hardesty mysteries.** 1998. Berkley, ISBN 0425166414, 288p.

A hard-boiled series featuring Vietnam vet turned California private eye Wil Hardesty. Hardesty would prefer to be building surfboards or out on the waves, but a strong ethical sense, and need for money, propels him to take on seemingly hopeless cases. Hardesty is a model of the introspective tough-guy PI. Here, he investigates an apparent suicide of a former 1960s radical and uncovers a host of skeletons.

Bruen, Ken
The Guards. **Jack Taylor series.** 2004. St. Martin's Minotaur, ISBN 0312320272, 304p.

Alcohol is a not uncommon solace for the tough-guy detective. And all too often the drinking takes on a life of its own. Drink was at the core of Bruen's Jack Taylor's firing from the Irish national police force, and he continues to drink heavily. His investigation into the apparent suicide of a friend's daughter leads to more violence, which is leavened somewhat by Taylor's sense of humor.

Connelly, Michael
Angels Flight. **Harry Bosch mysteries.** 2000. Warner Books, ISBN 0446607274, 480p.

Tough-guy investigators frequently follow their own code of justice that requires them to work on the edges of the letter of the law. For a private eye, this may not be so difficult, but Connelly's Harry Bosch is an LA cop, and his tactics often put him at odds with his superiors and colleagues. The pace is fast, and the violence realistic. In this entry in the series, Bosch investigates a racially motivated killing.

Hammett, Dashiell
⇨ *The Maltese Falcon*. 2005. Orion, ISBN 0752865331, 224p.

Sam Spade is one of the original tough guys, handy with a gun and with his fists, able to take a beating and come back, and imbued with a strong sense of honor. If you only know Spade from the movie, it is worth going back to the source to discover the model for so many tough guys to come. The San Francisco setting and the story of the stolen statue are as exciting now as when first published in the 1930s.

Hughes, Declan

Wrong Kind of Blood. 2006. William Morrow, ISBN 0060825464, 320p.

Declan Hughes's PI, Ed Loy, is about as far from the introspective detective as you can get. Loy is rough in both language and action, and the violence is equally graphic. An Irish expatriate living in California, Loy returns to Ireland to bury his mother. An old friend asks him to investigate her husband's disappearance, and when she turns up dead, Loy finds himself spiraling into the seamy side of Dublin in search of answers.

Jardine, Quintin

Skinner's Trail. **Bob Skinner mysteries.** 2001. Headline Book, ISBN 0747241414, 499p.

Edinburgh Deputy Chief Constable Bob Skinner is not the most sympathetic of detectives. There is an arrogant edge to his behavior, and Skinner is prone to take justice into his own hands as he sees fit. Skinner is no stranger to bloodshed in his police work, and he is more than able to handle himself in the violent Scottish underworld. Here, Skinner's investigation of the death of a Scottish drug lord leads him to Spain and crooked real estate dealing that may be related to the murder.

Vachss, Andrew

Blue Belle. **Burke mysteries.** 1995. Vintage, ISBN 0679761683, 352p.

Without a scorecard, you really cannot tell the good guys from the bad guys in Vachss's Burke stories. Burke is about as amoral as an investigator can get, and he does not hesitate to make decisions about who should die for their crimes. Accompanied by a gang of streetwise and violent sidekicks, Burke handles jobs that other detectives would walk away from. The stories are violent and often, as here, portray Burke taking on those who abuse children.

Baddest of the Bad: Crime's Worst Criminals

Where would all of these tough men and women be without their evil antagonists? Sometimes, the deranged or demonic criminal can be as compelling a figure in crime fiction as the detective is. Frequently, these monsters display intellectual capabilities that are the equal of their nemesis, but their hubris almost always brings them down in the end. The violence level is usually high in these stories, though sometimes the terror is more psychological than physical. Here are some of crime fiction's worst villains, wreaking their havoc on the innocent and peaceful.

Child, Lee
Tripwire. **Jack Reacher mysteries.** 2000. Jove, ISBN 0515128635, 432p.

Child's Jack Reacher is a former MP who is willing to take on investigations that others would just as soon let go. The stories are violent and dark, and Child has a knack for creating truly evil villains. Unexplained deaths, old and new, seem to all come back to a sinister loan shark, Hobie the Hook. The final confrontation between Hobie and Reacher is chilling and thrilling.

Connolly, John
Bad Men. 2005. Pocket, ISBN 0743487850, 480p.

The title says it all in this stand-alone novel that blends a police procedural with elements of the thriller and the supernatural. A seventeenth-century massacre haunts the lives of the modern villagers of Dutch Island, Maine. Now a vicious killer, Edward Moloch, spurred by ancestral memories of those earlier deaths, is headed toward the island bent on revenge. It's up to policeman Joe Dupree to stop him.

Holton, Hugh
Violent Crimes. **Larry Cole mysteries.** 1998. Forge, ISBN 0812571878, 512p.

Revenge is frequently at the center of these stories of evil. It can be real or imagined, but the criminal is often bent on making society (or an individual) pay for some perceived wrong. Holton's Larry Cole, a Chicago police detective, is faced with a malevolent millionaire, Steven Zalkin, who may also be a psychopathic killer from earlier in Cole's career.

Lindsay, Jeff
Darkly Dreaming Dexter. **Dexter mysteries.** 2005. Vintage, ISBN 1400095913, 304p.

Dexter Morgan is one of the most disturbing characters in crime fiction. A blood spatter expert who works for the Miami police, Dexter is also a violent and vicious serial killer. He is disturbingly normal in many ways, and as the narrator of the stories, Dexter is very aware of his dark side. But that does not stop him from following his urges to kill. The body counts are high, and the descriptions are gruesome, but there is also something strangely fascinating about Dexter.

McBain, Ed
Mischief. **87th Precinct mysteries.** 2003. Pocket, ISBN 0743463099, 480p.

McBain is known for his realistic, detailed, and very human portrayal of big-city policemen, set in a fictionalized New York City. Here, the 87th precinct cops are bedeviled by the appearance of their frequent adversary the "Deaf Man," who is leaving enigmatic clues to his forthcoming crime. McBain draws a chilling picture of evil as he shows the Deaf Man developing and implementing his plan.

Preston, Douglas, and Lincoln Child
⇨ *The Book of the Dead*. **Pendergast trilogy.** 2006. Warner Books, ISBN 0446576980, 464p.

A difficult childhood and a very bad relationship with his brother have left Diogenes Pendergast with a substantial animus toward FBI Special Agent Aloysius Pendergast. Unfortunately for Aloysius, Diogenes is not only sublimely evil, he is also a master plotter with no conscience. Aloysius needs all of his skills and intellect to survive Diogenes's hatred in this fast-paced entry in Preston and Child's trilogy.

Sandford, John
Night Prey. **Prey mysteries.** 2004. Berkley, ISBN 0425146413, 416p.

Sandford's Minneapolis police thrillers feature Detective Lucas Davenport, but the criminals in the stories are often equally and disturbingly as compelling as the good guys. Here, Davenport tracks down a powerfully evil serial killer who preys on young women. The narration alternates between following the killer and the pursuers, and the tension Sandford creates is palpable.

Through the Eyes of the Criminal

It is a short step from writing a crime novel with compelling and believable evildoers to making those rogues the focus of the story. There is something uncomfortably appealing about following the thoughts and actions of the criminal in a crime story. The stories in this list all feature lead characters who, if not actively engaged in criminal activities, are certainly operating on the edges of legality. Some of these stories are humorous and others darker and more violent, but readers looking to experience life on the edge will find much to like here.

Barger, Sonny
Dead in 5 Heartbeats. **Patch Kinkade mysteries.** 2004. HarperTorch, ISBN 006053253X, 304p.

Like his creator, Patch Kinkade has seemingly given up the violent life of a motorcycle gang leader. But when a member of his old gang is murdered, Kinkade feels bound to step in and investigate the killing and avenge the honor of the club. Barger offers a violent and profane entrée into the world of motorcycle gangs.

Block, Lawrence
⇨ *Hit Man*. **John Keller mysteries.** 1999. HarperTorch, ISBN 038072541X, 352p.

Frequently, crime fiction through the criminal's eyes presents the readers with a series of contrasts between the apparent normality of the criminal and the dark side that comes into view at times. This dark collection of linked stories features Keller living alone in the city, seeing his shrink, and worrying about his life. But Keller also travels the country killing people on contract. Block is a master of contradictions, and Keller is a memorable, if frightening, character.

Block, Lawrence

Burglars Can't Be Choosers. **Bernie Rhodenbarr mysteries.** 2004. Harper-Torch, ISBN 0060582553, 320p.

Block also has a lighter series of mysteries that looks at the world though criminal eyes. Bernie Rhodenbarr is a somewhat hapless burglar, who, in this initial book in the series, comes across a body in the apartment he is robbing. In order avoid having the killing pinned on him, Bernie must locate the real killers. This series offers a light and humorous take on the theme.

Campbell, David

Venetian Holiday. 2006. Thomas Dunne Books, ISBN 0312349904, 240p.

Another entry on the lighter side is Campbell's debut novel featuring enterprising art thief Kate Fujimori. In Venice on a commission to steal a copy of the Mona Lisa, Kate finds that another gang has nabbed the picture first, and to make matters worse, she is also being stalked by an assassin bent on revenge. The minutiae of the burglaries are fascinating, and Kate is an appealing character who can fight as well as burgle. She gets the opportunity to do both in this fast-paced, multilayered story.

Collins, Max

The Last Quarry. **Quarry mysteries.** 2006. Hard Case Crime, ISBN 0843955937, 201p.

For a more hard-boiled story, try Collins's series featuring hit man Quarry. Cold-blooded and ruthless, Quarry nonetheless has evinced some conscience over the years. Now more or less retired, he steps back in for one more job. But he violates the contract killer's first commandment, not to develop feelings for your target, and finds that emotions lead to jeopardy.

Dorsey, Tim

Hammerhead Ranch Motel. **Serge Storms mysteries.** 2001. HarperTorch, ISBN 0380732343, 384p.

Dorsey blends violence and humor in his stories of Florida serial killer and local history buff Serge Storms. Here, Serge and an assortment of other scoundrels are on the trail of a missing $5 million. Deaths abound, and Serge is at the bottom of many of them. But Dorsey's humor and his quirky characters keep this from being a completely bleak tale of greed and cruelty.

Westlake, Donald

The Hot Rock. **Dortmunder mysteries.** 2001. Mysterious Press, ISBN 0446677035, 304p.

Bumbling criminals usually don't make it past the end of the first novel, but Westlake's Dortmunder has been making his way through capers for 37 years. The pleasure here is in the details of setting up the heist, as Dortmunder, fresh out of prison, sets up the team and develops the scheme to steal a price-less emerald. But the initial theft goes awry, and Dortmunder and his crew make several more attempts.

Why Didn't They Ask the Cat (or the Dog)?: Pet Mysteries

Ever since the hound of the Baskervilles, animals have played a part in the annals of crime fiction. In addition to the giant hound that terrorizes the inhabitants of Baskerville Hall, the Sherlock Holmes stories contain examples of tracking dogs, the occasional viper, and a horse that kills a man, in which story Holmes remarks on the "curious incident of the dog in the night time." But was not until the late twentieth century that animals came to the forefront in the mystery story. Lillian Jackson Braun was among the first and best known with her cat stories. The titles in this list all have animals with at least costar billing in the story.

Albert, Susan Wittig
The Tale of Hill Top Farm. **Cottage Tales of Beatrix Potter.** 2005. Berkley, ISBN 0425201015, 304p.

> No one knew animals better than Beatrix Potter, whose tales of mice and ducks have delighted children of all ages. So it should not come as a surprise that when Potter turns to detection that the animals of the village play a crucial role in uncovering the solution. Although the villagers, and even newcomer Miss B. Potter, cannot understand the speech of their animal companions, the animals are adept at leading the humans to the clues they need to solve the mysterious death of a villager.

Babson, Marion
Nine Lives to Murder. 1995. St. Martin's Press, ISBN 0312955804, 192p.

> Babson is known for her stand-alone mysteries featuring all sorts of cats. *Nine Lives to Murder* features an ingenious plot twist. Shakespearean actor Win Fortesque falls from a ladder during a rehearsal. In the fall, he crashes into Monty, the theater cat, and somehow the two exchange con-sciousnesses. While Win's body makes a slow recovery with Monty in con-trol, his mind is on the prowl in Monty's body, looking for the person who attempted to kill him. Babson presents a clever tale with a lot of humor.

Benjamin, Carol Lea
This Dog for Hire. **Rachel Alexander and Dash mysteries.** 1997. Dell, ISBN 0440225205, 304p.

> Rachel Alexander is a PI in New York City, and she is accompanied in her work by her pit bull, Dashiell. Although Dash doesn't talk to the reader or

to Alexander, his sense for clues proves useful in the pair's investigations. Here, the team is asked to track down a hit-and-run driver who killed an artist and may have stolen his show dog. From the New York City art scene to the Westminster Kennel Club, Alexander and Dash are a great team.

Berenson, Laurien

Unleashed. **Melanie Travis mysteries.** 2001. Kensington, ISBN 1575666804, 272p.

Berenson's Melanie Travis is a poodle breeder and teacher who is looking forward to soon wedding her fiancé. But then his ex-wife moves to town to start at new magazine that will expose the dark side of the dog show world. Before the magazine is launched, the ex is dead, and Melanie is drawn into the investigation. With a keen eye for the show-dog business, Berenson's mysteries will delight dog lovers.

Braun, Lilian Jackson

The Cat Who Brought Down the House. **Cat Who mysteries.** 2003. Jove, ISBN 0515136557, 256p.

Braun is responsible for the cat-as-detective trend, starting off with two cozies in the 1960s featuring journalist Jim Qwilleran and his feline companions. She resurrected the series in the 1980s and is still going strong. Based in the town of Pickax in fictional Moose County (somewhere in the north-central United States), Qwill solves mysteries with the help of Koko and Yum Yum as well as the local librarian and his sometime flame Polly Duncan. Here, an aging Hollywood star returns to her hometown, only to be bedeviled by family secrets and possible murder. The characters, human and feline, are the real draw in Braun's books.

Brown, Rita Mae

⇨ *Wish You Were Here*. **Mrs. Murphy mysteries.** 1991. Bantam, ISBN 0553287532, 320p.

Many of the feline detectives have to use their wits to nudge their human companions toward the clues. In Brown's series, Mrs. Murphy, a cat, and Tucker, a Corgi, at least can work with each other to point their owner in the right direction. Crozet, Virginia, postmistress Mary Minor Haristeen is fortunate in her pets as they assist her in uncovering the secrets behind the deaths of local businessmen who received mysterious postcards just prior to being killed. The conversations between the cat and dog are hilarious.

Henry, Sue

Tooth of Time. **Maxie and Stretch mysteries.** 2007. Onyx, ISBN 0451412370, 288p.

A widow, her dachshund, and a Winnebago roll into town. It sounds like the start of a bad joke, but actually it is the start of a fine series. Maxie McNabb is an appealing character, as is her dog, Stretch. Maxie arrives in Taos, New Mexico, and becomes acquainted with a woman who may have recently tried to kill herself. After a visit to Maxie's RV, the woman disappears and is later discovered with her wrists slit. But Maxie is suspicious of the suicide verdict, especially after her vehicle is ransacked. Stretch has a strong sense of good and evil and is a faithful companion in Maxie's investigations.

Chapter Three

Setting

For many readers, setting is an essential part of the reading experience. This can be particularly true of crime fiction, where some readers are drawn to stories placed in urban settings with all of their associated hustle and bustle, whereas other readers may look for more isolated locales for their mysteries. Choice of setting offers us the opportunity to visit exotic places where we have never been before or to come back to the streets that we could walk blindfolded. Setting encompasses not only the geographic location of the story but also the time period in which it is set. The recent boom in historical crime fiction has widely expanded the range of possibilities, and we can now find detection being done from the age of the pharaohs to modern times. The lists offered in this chapter all feature writers who can capture the feel and sense of a particular location or time period. These are mysteries that will take you places. The lists begin with a series of chronologically grouped mystery stories and then progress to the varied geographic and cultural settings.

Classical Way of Death: From Ancient Egypt to Early Greece and Rome

Although the idea of a civil police force did not really come into being until the eighteenth and nineteenth centuries, murder goes back to the days of Cain and Abel. Of course, in that case the culprit was pretty obvious, but other early murders required the services of those people whose native wit and powers of observation made them useful to both the rich and powerful and sometimes to the lowly as well. The titles here feature the best of these early masters of detection, from the pharaonic dynasties through the period following the fall of Rome.

Apostolou, Anna
   Murder in Macedon. **Alexander the Great mysteries.** 1998. St. Martin's Paperbacks, ISBN 0312967926, 272p.

   The murder of Philip of Macedon, father of Alexander the Great, leaves Alexander himself under some suspicion of arranging the killing. In order to dispel the rumors and solidify his authority, Alexander commands two of his servants, Miriam and Simeon, to investigate the circumstances around Philip's death. Apostolou, a pseudonym for the prolific historical mystery writer P. C. Doherty, has created a believable blend of political intrigue and mystery.

Davis, Lindsey
   The Silver Pigs. **Marcus Didius Falco mysteries.** 2006. St. Martin's Minotaur, ISBN 031235777X, 352p.

   Davis manages to bring the sensibility of a hard-boiled PI novel to ancient Rome and carries it off without losing any of the historical appeal. Falco is a rough-hewn character who enjoys women and wine but also has a sense of honor. The humor is broad, but Davis does not flinch from showing the dark side of Roman life, as in this story in which Falco ends up working as a slave in a Roman silver mine as part of his investigation.

Doherty, P. C.
   The Mask of Ra. **Egyptian mysteries.** 2001. Berkley, ISBN 042518093X, 288p.

   Writing under his own name here, Doherty begins a new series set in the fifteenth century B.C.E., the time of Pharaoh Tuthmosis. When Tuthmosis dies at the height of his power, the power struggles begin in the Egyptian court. The chief judge of Thebes, Amerotke, must step in to identify the killer and restore the peace. Doherty brings a great sense of court life in early Egypt to the story and makes good use of his knowledge of Egyptian religion and medicine.

Reed, Mary, and Eric Mayer
   One for Sorrow. **John the Eunuch mysteries.** 1999. Poisoned Pen Press, ISBN 1890208191, 292p.

   Where better to set a mystery series than in Byzantium, the place that became a byword for political intrigue and gamesmanship? Reed and Mayer create a realistic picture of life in sixth-century Byzantium and of the religious and political turmoil of the time. Here, the investigations are carried on by John the Eunuch, chamberlain to Emperor Justinian. The mystery is well crafted, and the secondary characters add to the strong sense of place.

Roberts, John Maddox

SPQR: The King's Gambit. **Decius Caecilius Metellus mysteries.** 1990. St. Martin's
Minotaur, ISBN 0312277059, 288p.

The annals of Rome are bloody indeed, as anyone who has read *I, Claudius*
can attest. A well-born investigator has much to keep him busy in the early days
of the Republic, as young Roman civil servant Decius Caecilius Metellus discovers. Metellus's investigations of a series of seemingly unconnected deaths
uncover political corruption at high levels, and the portraits of historical characters such as Julius Caesar and Cicero add to the atmosphere.

Robinson, Lynda

⇨ *Murder in the Place of Anubis*. **Lord Meren mysteries.** 1994. Fawcett, ISBN
0345389220, 224p.

King Tut has come to the throne, but his position is precarious. The intersection of religion and politics can lead to the rise of fanaticism that threat-
ens the young king. Fortunately, Tut has Lord Meren, the Eyes and the Ears
of Pharaoh, to keep alert to threats. Robinson deftly displays her knowledge
of the customs and traditions of ancient Egypt and paints a realistic picture of
Egyptian life in the fourteenth century B.C.E. In this first title, Meren investigates the murder of a royal scribe.

Saylor, Steven

Roman Blood. **Gordianus the Finder mysteries.** 2000. St. Martin's Minotaur,
ISBN 0312972962, 416p.

Darker in tone than many historical mysteries, Saylor's series probably
comes closest to the precarious realities of life in Rome in the first century
B.C.E. Like many of his fellow classical investigators, Gordianus finds himself
caught up in the political infighting that marked this period. Over the course of
his investigations, Gordianus encounters a wide range of historical characters,
from Cicero to Catalina to Caesar, and Saylor's depiction of them and their
roles in Rome's history always rings true. In this first title, Gordianus is hired
by Cicero to investigate a killing in which Cicero is defending the accused.

Serf and Turf: Medieval Mysteries

As the centuries turned, there came a sense that the civil authorities should
have an increased role in the prevention of crime. The development of the sheriff and his ancillary officers prefigures the eventual establishment of a police
force. But the officials involved in keeping the peace often take the easiest solution to a crime, not necessarily the correct one. So it is fortunate that a host of
amateur detectives seem to have flourished during the Middle Ages. In occupations that range from peddler to religious, these sleuths shed some light during
the Dark Ages.

Doherty, P. C.

The Crown in Darkness. **Hugh Corbett mysteries.** 1991. Headline Book, ISBN 0747235058, 192p.

In the days of King Edward I, England's relations with Scotland were tenuous at best. When King Alexander III of Scotland dies of a fall, Hugh Corbett, clerk to the chancellor of England, takes on the investigation. His prying leads to a variety of violent attempts on his life. Doherty's series is rich with descriptions of England and Scotland in the fourteenth century and is based on historical events.

Gordon, Alan

Thirteenth Night. **Fools' Guild mysteries.** 2000. St. Martin's Minotaur, ISBN 0312976844, 256p.

Traveling entertainers have entry into the palaces and homes of rulers and would-be rulers, so it only seems logical that the Fool's Guild takes on responsibility for manipulating events to keep the peace across Europe and Byzantium. The first in the series is sort of a sequel to Shakespeare's *Twelfth Night,* with the fool Theophilis (Feste) taking the main role. The stories offer fascinating detail of the thirteenth century in a lighter vein that includes a fair dash of humor. The Near East settings for several of the tales add additional interest.

Grace, C. L.

Saintly Murders. **Kathryn Swinbrooke mysteries.** 2001. St. Martin's Minotaur, ISBN 0312269935, 256p.

Medieval apothecaries have a familiarity with death that makes them prime candidates for detecting when crimes are discovered. One of the most appealing of this group is apothecary Kathryn Swinbrooke. With her companion Colum Murtagh, master of the king's horse, Swinbrooke puts her knowledge of herbs and a sharp eye for clues to good use in the investigation of the death of a friar in fifteenth-century Canterbury.

Jecks, Michael

Mad Monk of Gidleigh. **Medieval West Country mysteries.** 2005. Headline Book, ISBN 0755301692, 480p.

In contrast to the host of amateur detectives on this list, Jecks presents a couple of protopolicemen, Baldwin Furnshill, Keeper of the King's Peace and former Knight Templar, and Simon Puttock, bailiff of Lydford Castle. An appealing pair, here the two investigate the murder of a local girl, who it turns out was pregnant. Jecks ably contrasts the lives of the wealthy and the poor in these detailed mysteries.

Levack, Simon

Demon of the Air. **Aztec mysteries.** 2005. St. Martin's Minotaur, ISBN 0312348347, 320p.

In a fascinating and disturbing tale, Levack sets his mystery in the court of Montezuma, in the period just prior to the arrival of the Spanish conquistadors.

A botched human sacrifice—the victim killed himself first—brings the slave Yaotl to the attention of the emperor, whose dreams are troubled with strange visions. Yaotl is given the task of uncovering the plots behind the suicide and discovers a tangled web of conspiracies.

Marston, Edward
The Wolves of Savernake. **Gervase Bret and Ralph Delchard mysteries.** 1995. Fawcett, ISBN 0449223108, 243p.

In the time of William the Conqueror, relations between the newly arrived Normans and the defeated Saxons were strained. The king has sent a Norman noble and a young Saxon clerk to investigate claims against an abbey, and when the claimant is found dead, they must dig into the past to uncover the killer. Marston, who writes other historical mysteries, has an ear for dialogue and a commanding knowledge of eleventh-century England.

Robb, Candace
The Nun's Tale. **Owen Archer mysteries.** 1996. St. Martin's Paperbacks, ISBN 0312959826, 355p.

Robb's series features the one-eyed military man Owen Archer, now in service to the archbishop of York. Intrigue, political and religious, is Robb's stock in trade, and she has an excellent understanding of the role of religion, both spiritual and political, in fourteenth-century England. Here, Archer is called on to look into the resurrection of a nun, who is discovered living after she has supposedly died and been buried.

Roe, Caroline
⇨ *Remedy for Treason*. **Isaac of Girona mysteries.** 1998. Berkley, ISBN 0425162958, 259p.

Although most of the medieval mysteries are set in England, Roe's books take you into Spain in the fourteenth century. An accomplished medievalist, Roe makes this world come to life through her descriptive style and her strong characters. Isaac of Girona is a Jewish physician who serves as physician and investigator for the archbishop of Girona. The stories have an interesting blend of royal politics and religion and start with this tale of the plague and a plot to overthrow the Spanish monarchy.

Sedley, Kate
Death and the Chapman. **Roger the Chapman mysteries.** 1992. St. Martin's Press, ISBN 0312069456, 190p.

Roger the Chapman is one of the most amiable of medieval sleuths. Having given up on a monastic career, Roger is happiest out on the road, selling from his pack. His peregrinations give Sedley ample opportunity to depict the lives of rich and poor alike in fifteenth-century England. Trouble seems to follow Roger, though, and here he is drawn into the search for three missing persons, whose disappearances may or may not be connected.

Ours Is Not to Reason Why:
Crime in the Age of Enlightenment

As the Renaissance blossomed and the world left the darkness of the medieval period, detection also changed. New techniques are added to the resources of the detective as an increased understanding of the workings of the body begins to allow more forensic evidence to be considered. A more formal policing effort, provided by the state, comes to the fore. Then the age of reason ushered in a reliance on the intellect and a moving away from superstition. At the same time, the arsenal of the criminal expands, and new weapons and more sophisticated crimes seem to spring up across the period. One constant remains, though, the need for observant investigators, able to make the connections that allow them to solve a multitude of crimes. Here you will find the most rational sleuths from the Renaissance through the Age of Reason.

Alexander, Bruce

⇨*Blind Justice*. **Sir John Fielding mysteries.** 1995. Berkley, ISBN 0425150070, 336p.

Sir John Fielding was the blind magistrate of the Bow Street Court and brother of Tom Fielding, novelist and founder of the Bow Street Runners, England's first real police force. Alexander's novels capture all the elements you want in a historical mystery: strong characters, a feel for the sights and sounds of the period (eighteenth-century London, in this case), and a clever puzzle. If you want a sense of the legal and criminal justice systems of eighteenth-century England, look no farther. This first book in the series introduces Fielding and his helper, young orphan Jeremy Proctor, as they unravel the death of Lord Goodhope.

Buckley, Fiona

To Shield the Queen. **Ursula Blanchard mysteries.** 1998. Pocket, ISBN 0671015311, 336p.

Buckley sets her series in the court of Elizabeth I, in a time of political and religious intrigue and plotting. Ursula Blanchard is a lady-in-waiting to the queen, but she also works as an investigator for Elizabeth's secretary of state, William Cecil. Buckley makes the most of the conflict raised over religious differences in England at this time. In the first entry in the series, Mistress Blanchard is sent to keep an eye on the wife of Robert Dudley, whose death would pave the course for her husband to marry the queen. In a story based on historical facts, Buckley deftly blends history and fiction into a seamless mystery.

Chisholm, P. F.

A Famine of Horses. **Sir Robert Carey mysteries.** 1999. Poisoned Pen Press, ISBN 1890208272, 400p.

The court of Elizabeth I provides the backdrop for Chisholm's series. Robert Carey is appointed deputy warden of the West March, protecting England's

Scottish border. Carey has to deal not only with local Scots raiding over the border but also the threat of a more substantial invasion from Scotland. Filled with period detail, Chisholm's stories take the reader to the troubled and atmospheric borderlands, and he has a great ear for the language of the period.

Eyre, Elisabeth
An Axe for an Abbot. **Sigismondo mysteries.** 1996. St. Martin's Press, ISBN 031213925X, 339p.

Eyre (a pseudonym for a team of mystery writers) chooses a unique setting for her mystery series: Renaissance Italy, the heart of intellectual development. The stories feature hired swordsman Sigismondo, odd-job man for the duke of Rocca. Eyre's tale ranges from high life to low, and she does not shy from the dark side of life. Here, Sigismondo vows to deliver a jeweled cross to a shrine, but a series of murders intervenes, and he needs to unravel them before he can complete his mission.

Hall, Robert Lee
Benjamin Franklin Takes the Case. **Benjamin Franklin mysteries.** 2001. Pine Street Books, ISBN 0812217896, 227p.

Prior to the American Revolution, Benjamin Franklin spent much time in London as the agent of the colonies. When he arrives to visit a fellow printer, Franklin finds the shop in turmoil, his friend dead, and 12-year-old Nicholas Handy bereft of his apprenticeship. The pair take up the investigation, and Hall puts Franklin's skills to good use. An intriguing puzzle and a host of fictional and historical characters make this series a great introduction to mid-eighteenth-century London.

Liss, David
A Spectacle of Corruption. **Benjamin Weaver mysteries.** 2004. Random House, ISBN 0375508554, 384p.

Liss's literary and detailed mysteries are set on the edges of society in eighteenth-century London. Former prizefighter Benjamin Weaver is now working as a thief-taker, but someone wants him out of the way, and he is framed and arrested. Following his escape, Weaver traverses the city from the coffeehouses and taverns to the homes of the wealthy to clear his name and discover the real criminal. Liss captures London in all its filth and splendor, and he has a sharp ear for the language of both high and low society.

Marston, Edward
The Queen's Head. **Nicholas Bracewell mysteries.** 2000. Poisoned Pen Press, ISBN 1890208450, 194p.

Marston sets his delightful series in an Elizabethan theater company. Lord Westfield's Men eke out a precarious existence as a London acting troupe. Much of the pleasure in the stories comes from the rivalries within the company and between Westfield's Men and the other companies. The novels are replete with details of Elizabethan theater. Nicholas Bracewell, the manager of Westfield's Men, is an appealing sleuth, and here he must unravel a plot to both destroy the company and attack the queen, who will be coming to see a command performance.

Rowland, Laura Joh

Shinju. **Sano Ichiro mysteries.** 1996. HarperTorch, ISBN 0061009504, 448p.

If you want to venture beyond the usual Elizabethan setting, Rowland's series set in seventeenth-century Tokyo is sure to please. The series stars Sano Ichiro, most honorable investigator of events, situations, and people for the shogun. Propelled by a strong sense of honor and justice, Sano risks his profession and life to discover the truth behind an apparent double suicide. The description of seventeenth-century Japan is rich and believable, and later titles in the series introduce Sano's wife, who is an equally compelling character.

The Queen Is Not Amused: Victorian Sleuthing

The Victorian period is noted for its strict social codes and harsh punishments for those who violate those standards. The development of formal police forces and private investigators beginning in the late eighteenth century provides fertile ground for writers of historical mysteries. Increasing sophistication of crime scene and medical techniques also gives the detectives a wider range of options to use in solving crimes. At the same time, societal changes offer writers a wide range of options for their central mysteries. Expanding roles for women, industrialization, and the shrinking of the globe in light of transportation advances all come into play in these stories. From the Regency period through the end of Victoria's lengthy reign and into Edwardian days, detection flourishes in this list.

Akunin, Boris

Sister Pelagia and the White Bulldog. **Sister Pelagia mysteries.** 2007. Random House, ISBN 0812975138, 288p.

Orthodox Bishop Mishenka Mitrofanii has a reputation for cleverness in unraveling difficult questions. But in reality, it is the observant, but unremarkable, Sister Pelagia who is the investigator. The mystery is seamlessly blended with a lively and humorous portrayal of life in late nineteenth-century Russia. The bishop sends Pelagia to look into a series of deaths on his grandmother's estate, including her prized bulldogs.

Alleyn, Susanne

Game of Patience. 2006. St. Martin's Minotaur, ISBN 0312343639, 304p.

The Reign of Terror is over, but France is still unsettled, and that Corsican is still leading the French army in Italy. In Paris, a young woman of a well-positioned family is found dead along with the man who was blackmailing her. It falls to a sometime police spy, Aristide Ravel, to investigate the deaths. Alleyn blends the standard elements of a historical mystery—interesting detail of post-Revolution France and a strong sense of place—with the form of a police procedural as Ravel investigates a variety of possible suspects.

Chesney, Marion

Our Lady of Pain. **Harry Cathcart mysteries.** 2006. St. Martin's Paperbacks, ISBN 0312998007, 224p.

Chesney is a master at depicting the social snobbery of the Edwardian period in this lighthearted series. Captain Cathcart is a rather ne'er-do-well former soldier who finds income and pleasure in fixing situations for the upper class. The stories mix a strong element of romance with the mystery, with Cathcart having an engagement of convenience with Lady Rose Summer that seems to become increasingly real for the pair. A delightful look into English high society in the early twentieth century.

Dickinson, David

Goodnight Sweet Prince. **Lord Francis Powerscourt mysteries.** 2002. Carroll and Graf, ISBN 0786709456, 314p.

The veneer of respectability of the lives of the eminent Victorians was sometimes very thin, and there is a dark undercurrent in the period that Dickinson ably captures in his series. In this first entry, Lord Powerscourt, known for his discreet handling of sensitive military investigations, is recruited to look into possible blackmail of the royal family. But then Prince Eddy, grandson of Victoria and son of the eventual Edward VI, is found murdered. The prince's dissolute lifestyle offers a variety of reasons for his death, and Powerscourt must sort out the truth. The book seamlessly mixes history and fiction into an exciting mystery.

Monfredo, Miriam

Seneca Falls Inheritance. **Glynis Tryon mysteries.** 1994. Berkley, ISBN 0425144658, 304p.

The struggle for women's emancipation in the United States began in Seneca Falls, New York, in the 1840s. The First Women's Rights Convention provides the backdrop for the story as librarian Glynis Tryon investigates the killing of a young woman who may have been the daughter of a wealthy townsman who has recently died. Monfredo uses the historical details of the period carefully in building a believable world.

Perry, Anne

Defend and Betray. **William Monk and Hester Latterly mysteries.** 1993. Ivy Books, ISBN 080411188X, 448p.

Few writers capture the dark edges of nineteenth-century England like Anne Perry. Perry frequently centers her mysteries around social issues of the day, giving her the opportunity to explore the underbelly of Victorian life. Perry's investigators, nurse Hester Latterly and former policeman William Monk, are an interesting pair, and the novels are filled with a secondary cast of characters that brings London to life.

Ross, Kate
⇨ *Cut to the Quick*. **Julian Kestrel mysteries.** 1994. Penguin, ISBN 0140233946, 352p.

Ross's Julian Kestrel prefigures Dorothy Sayers's Lord Peter Wimsey by about a century. Kestrel is a well-known member of London society in the Regency period, but he is more than a rakish member of the upper class. With the help of his manservant, a former pickpocket, Kestrel is as adept a detective as he is a dandy. Ross has an excellent eye for Regency details, and the mystery, a death at a wedding, offers a compelling tale.

Thomas, Will
Some Danger Involved. **Cyrus Baker and Thomas Llewelyn mysteries.** 2005. Touchstone, ISBN 0743256190, 304p.

If you like the Holmesian feel of a dark and brooding London, full of fogs and smokes, then try Thomas's Baker and Llewelyn series. Cyrus Baker is a private investigator, and his assistant, Thomas Llewelyn, was expelled from Oxford. The pair investigates a killing in London's Jewish quarter in the opening novel in this highly atmospheric series.

Samurai Spade: Murder in the Far East

In early crime fiction, the Far East was viewed as a birthplace of exotic poisons and evil masterminds who spread their web of terror across the "civilized" world. Fortunately, mystery writers take a more reasoned approach to the East these days, and mysteries set in China, Japan, Korea, and other Asian Pacific countries can be read for their fascinating descriptions of Eastern culture and traditions. This list covers a range of times and locations, but all the titles give an insight into the life and customs of the countries on the Pacific Rim.

Church, James
A Corpse in the Koryo. 2006. Thomas Dunne, ISBN 0312352085, 288p.

A police state makes for an intriguing setting for a work of crime fiction, and Church's novel, set in North Korea, offers a unique look at that bleak and oppressive society. Inspector O is an honest, if cynical, officer of the state security forces. He is given an apparently routine assignment that ends up spiraling into a full-blown conspiracy of corruption, political maneuvering, and danger.

Cotterill, Colin

The Coroner's Lunch. **Dr. Paiboun mysteries.** 2005. Soho Crime, ISBN 1569474184, 272p.

Following the Communist takeover of Laos, doctors are in short supply, and Siri Paiboun, who had been looking forward to retiring, is pressed into service as the national coroner. Cotterill mixes politics, some humor, and a bit of the supernatural here as Dr. Paiboun investigates the death of a party member's wife. Cotterill paints a sympathetic picture of Laos and its people, from the city to the countryside.

Gulik, Robert

The Phantom of the Temple. **Judge Dee mysteries.** 1995. University of Chicago Press, ISBN 0226848779, 214p.

Gulik's Judge Dee series is set in imperial China in the seventh century C.E. In the tales, Gulik mined his knowledge of the Ming Dynasty period for details of law, literature, and day-to-day life to increase the believability of the stories. There is a certain level of gruesomeness in the tales, with beheadings and other violent crimes making appearances. Here, Judge Dee ties together three seemingly disconnected cases in China's western frontier.

Pattison, Eliot

The Skull Mantra. **Shan Tao Yun mysteries.** 2001. St. Martin's Paperbacks, ISBN 0312978340, 448p.

Former Chinese police inspector Shan Toa Yin has been dismissed from service and sentenced to a work camp in the Tibetan mountains. It is a harsh existence in which prisoners are beaten and killed for the least infractions. Pattison captures both the cruelty of the camp and its officers and the awe-inspiring beauty of Tibet. When a work crew discovers a body, the camp's sadistic commander brings Shan into the investigation.

Rowland, Laura Joh

The Concubine's Tattoo. **Sano Ichiro mysteries.** 2000. St. Martin's Paperbacks, ISBN 0312969228, 376p.

Rowland convincingly re-creates seventeenth-century Tokyo in this series featuring Sano Ichiro, Most Honorable Investigator of Events, Situations, and People for the shogun. Rowland understands not only the details of daily life but also the larger concepts of service and honor that formed the foundation of the shogun system. In this entry, Sano investigates the death of one of the shogun's concubines and at the same time must deal with his new marriage and his wife's interest in the investigation.

See, Lisa

➪ *Dragon Bones*. **Liu Hulan and David Stark mysteries.** 2004. Ballantine, ISBN 0345440315, 368p.

Set in contemporary China, See's series offers great insight into the current political and cultural upheavals there. Here, See's detecting team, Ministry of Public Security Inspector Liu Hulan and her husband, U.S. lawyer David Stark, is sent to the site of the Three Rivers Gorge dam to investigate the murder of a U.S. archaeologist and the theft of artifacts from the site. The story involves religion, history, culture, and a satisfying mystery.

Death in Venice, and Other Travel Hot Spots

Just like readers in every genre, we crime fiction fans not only read for the puzzle but also to be taken to new places. Interesting settings, especially ones that we might not be able to visit in person, often are a draw for readers. When reading mystery fiction, it is interesting to note how often the best stories are like a piece of fine jewelry, with a precious stone, the mystery, placed in a wonderful setting that enhances its luster. All of the stories here are set in locations that are destinations for tourists and travelers of all sorts. Sometimes the story involves these wanderers, but as often, the location simply provides a glorious setting for crime.

Abel, Kenneth

Cold Steel Rain. **Danny Chaisson mysteries**. 2000. Putnam, ISBN 0399146628, 448p.

> One of the pleasures of reading crime fiction set in interesting locales is the opportunity to see behind the standard tourist view of the city. Abel takes us into the dreary and sometimes scary parts of the Big Easy in his New Orleans–based mysteries featuring former District Attorney Danny Chaisson. Abel's New Orleans is more than the bars and voodoo shops of the French Quarter, Mardi Gras, and the beautiful houses of the Garden District. He brings to life all of the city and its varied inhabitants.

Black, Cara

Murder in the Marais. **Aimee Leduc mysteries.** 2000. Soho, ISBN 1569472122, 360p.

> Black has a great feel for both the city and the people of Paris, and she brings the "city of light" to life in her Aimee Leduc mysteries. Leduc is a tough, fearless PI, specializing in computer crimes, who here is caught up in Paris's past when a murder seems to link neo-Nazi activity to secrets from Paris's Jewish community in World War II. Black captures the smells and sounds of Paris in this atmospheric series.

Henry, Sue

The Tooth of Time. Maxie and Stretch mysteries. 2007. Onyx, ISBN 0451412370, 288p.

> Taos, New Mexico, has been an artist colony and tourist destination for almost a century now and still attracts travelers for its skiing, its art galleries,

and its southwestern atmosphere. Although there is not much skiing in Henry's mystery, she does capture the feel of the Southwest and the artistic endeavors of the citizens of Taos. Maxie McNabb and her dachshund, Stretch, are an appealing pair in this delightful cozy.

Jeffries, Roderic
An Artistic Way to Go. **Inspector Alvarez mysteries.** 1997. St. Martin's Press, ISBN 0312154720, 188p.

The Mediterranean island of Mallorca is home to three distinct groups, the native islanders, a large community of British expatriates, and hordes of tourists. Responsible for all of these groups is Enrique Alvarez, the long-suffering police inspector. The appeal here is in the descriptions of the island and its people as much as in the mystery story. Sun-drenched Mallorca comes to life in this long-standing series.

Leon, Donna
⇨ *Blood from a Stone*. **Guido Brunetti mysteries.** 2006. Penguin, ISBN 014303698X, 384p.

Few writers are as adept as Leon at capturing a city in all its seasons and decaying splendors. The city of Venice is always a presence in the story: its cafés and restaurants, its canals and streets, the shops and factories, and the homes of its people. Commisaire Brunetti has a deep love for his native town, and his affection for Venice and her people compel his search for justice. This series entry finds Brunetti investigating the killing of an African guest worker and raises the issues of immigration, legal and illegal, and tourism in Venice.

Riggs, Cynthia
Jack in the Pulpit. **Victoria Trumbull mysteries.** 2004. St. Martin's Minotaur, ISBN 0312330111, 224p.

Martha's Vineyard is a popular vacation destination, but life on the island does not close down when the wealthy tourists leave their compounds at the end of summer. Riggs's cozy series featuring Victoria Trumbull, a 92-year old grandmother and deputy for the West Tisbury police, centers on the lives of those people for whom the Vineyard is a permanent home. This series entry tells of Trumbull's first foray into crime solving as a feud between ministers stirs up the community. The mysteries are always interesting, and Riggs brings a sharp eye for the natural beauty of the island that makes Martha's Vineyard such an appealing spot.

Ripley, J. R.
Murder in St. Barts. **Gendarme Trenet mysteries.** 2003. Beachfront, ISBN 1892339552, 247p.

Saint Barthélemy, in the French West Indies, is noted for its white-sand beaches and volcanic mountains. A small, French-speaking community of 7,000 lives on the island, but the majority population is tourists, with celebrities leading the vanguard. Keeping the peace here is Gendarme Charles Trenet, who is expecting few difficulties. But when a rich American is killed, Trenet must take over the investigation. Local color and an appealing detective make this a fun read.

Tallis, Frank
  A Death in Vienna. **Liebermann mysteries.** 2006. Grove, ISBN 0802118151, 464p.

   As the nineteenth century turned into the twentieth, Vienna, Austria, was a center for intellectual and cultural life. The cafés and coffeehouses were hotbeds for discussing politics, art, and society in general. Tallis re-creates this thriving community in his historical mysteries featuring psychoanalyst Max Liebermann. With his detective comrade, Liebermann is drawn into the investigation of the mysterious death of a medium.

To the Manor Born: Country House Mysteries

The English country house mystery has been a staple of crime fiction almost since the genre's inception. These stories offer the author an isolated and often fascinating setting for the crime and offer the reader a look into the darker side of high society. Sometimes the butler did it, and other times it is the manor house owner, but in all cases, the titles listed here are set in the opulent world of the country house.

Bebris, Carrie
  Pride and Prescience. **Mr. and Mrs. Darcy mysteries.** 2005. Tor Books, ISBN 0765350718, 288p.

   In the spirit of Jane Austen, Bebris's series follows the life of Fitzwilliam and Elizabeth Darcy after their wedding. The couple finds themselves investigating a series of strange occurrences involving Caroline Bingley, sister of Elizabeth's brother-in-law Charles. Their inquiries take them to Netherfield, Charles's county estate, where more trouble ensues. Bebris ably captures the style and feel of Austen's characters and setting.

Christie, Agatha
  ⇨ *Hercule Poirot's Christmas*. **Hercule Poirot mysteries**. 2001. HarperCollins, ISBN 0007120699, 336p.

   Christie is the acknowledged queen of the English manor house mystery. She has a feel for the daily functioning of the household and for the strict lines between upstairs and downstairs that governed this world. Here, her pre-eminent sleuth, Hercule Poirot, is invited to Gorston Hall for Christmas and discovers a puzzling mystery when the master of the hall is killed in his own bedroom, which is locked on the inside.

Dickinson, David
Death Called to the Bar. **Lord Francis Powerscourt mysteries.** 2006. Carroll and Graf, ISBN 0786719990, 256p.

Powerscourt is a solver of problems for the Victorian upper class. Here, the deaths of two lawyers take him from the legal precincts of London to the country estate of one of the dead men. Powerscourt discovers that the sealed-off rooms of the estate contain more than just old-master paintings and dusty furniture. Dickinson has a fine sense of life in the Victorian period and an eye for detail that wins readers.

Dunn, Carola
The Gunpowder Plot. **Daisy Dalrymple mysteries.** 2006. St Martin's Minotaur, ISBN 0312349890, 272p.

Dunn takes us back to the apogee of the English country house, the 1920s, just after World War I. Dunn's heroine, reporter Daisy Dalrymple, comes to Edge Manor, home of a school friend, to write about the family's annual Guy Fawkes celebrations. When her friend's father turns up dead, part of an apparent murder-suicide, Daisy calls in her husband, Inspector Alec Fletcher, to help sort out the skeletons in the estate's closets.

Emerson, Kathy
Face Down Below the Banqueting House. **Lady Susanna Appleton mysteries.** 2005. Perseverance Press, ISBN 1880284715, 240p.

There's no reason that a good manor house mystery needs to be set in modern times. After all, many of the great estates date back to the time of the Tudors. Elizabeth I is reigning, and well-born herbalist, Susanna Appleton is making arrangements for the court to visit Leigh Abbey when a death occurs. Lady Susanna must determine if it was an accident or something more sinister. Emerson knows the period and brings the occupants of a sixteenth-century manor house to life.

Kingsbury, Kate
A Bicycle Built for Murder. **Manor House mysteries.** 2001. Berkley, ISBN 0425178560, 216p.

Kingsbury captures the rhythms of life in the rural English village of Sitting Marsh during World War II. Village life centers around Manor House and its mistress, 31-year-old Elizabeth Hartleigh Compton, who takes on responsibility for the local inhabitants and their worries. So when a teenage girl, known for her promiscuous behavior, goes missing, Compton steps in to find her. The characters and the setting make this series a delightful addition to the field.

Paige, Robin
Death at Glamis Castle. **Kate and Charles Sheridan mysteries.** 2004. Berkley, ISBN 0425192644, 352p.

Ever since Macbeth, Glamis Castle has had a bad name. When King Edward asks Lord Charles Sheridan and his wife, novelist Kate, to investigate a death at the castle in the early 1900s, they find more mysteries than they bargained for. Paige has a grand sense of English aristocratic life, and the castle itself becomes a character.

Death in the Big City: Urban Crimes and Misdemeanors

The density of people and the frenetic pace of urban life offer mystery writers a broad palate with which to work. Contemporary urban crime fiction frequently focuses on the economic desolation in the inner city and the desperation of the people who live there. The brooding streets and sunless avenues echo this desperation. These are often dark tales without much hope of redemption. Whether they are police procedurals or feature private investigators, these tales from the city offer a grim, but realistic, view of crime in an urban setting.

Case, Dave
Out of Cabrini. **Stacey Macbeth mysteries.** 2006. Five Star, ISBN 1594143781, 339p.

> In the annals of crime, Chicago is best known for mobsters and corrupt politicians. But a sprawling housing project, Cabrini Green, is home to a more personal and frightening brand of criminal activity. Violent gangs involved in the drug trade control Cabrini and exact revenge on those who cross them. Chicago policeman Stacey Macbeth and his colleagues on the tactical team are responsible for trying to keep the peace. As a former Chicago police officer, Case knows the city and its people.

Chandler, Raymond
⇨ *Lady in the Lake*. **Philip Marlowe mysteries.** 1988. Vintage, ISBN 0394758250, 272p.

> Chandler is revered by many as the best writer of hard-boiled private eye stories, and Marlowe has become the paradigm for generations of tough but sensitive PIs. In addition to a memorable prose style and compelling characters, Chandler is equally well known for his descriptions of Los Angeles in the 1940s. The city, in all its sun-blessed splendor, is a main character in all of Chandler's books, and Marlowe is intimately familiar with the bright and the dark sides of the City of Angels. Here, he investigates the disappearances of two women.

Hunsicker, Harry
Still River. **Lee Henry Oswald mysteries.** 2005. St. Martin's Minotaur, ISBN 0312337876, 288p.

> As the twentieth century closed and the twenty-first century opened, the world of the PI expanded beyond the usual mean streets of the costal cities of

New York, San Francisco, and LA. A tough Dallas PI, Oswald is the center of this fast-paced and violent story. The oil boom has brought prosperity to Dallas, but not everyone has benefited, and Hunsicker, a Dallas native, knows the stories from both sides of the street.

Jackson, John A.

Hit on the House. **Detective Sergeant Mulheisen mysteries.** 2000. Grove Press, ISBN 0802137059, 256p.

The city streets and the old neighborhoods of Detroit are the beat for Detective Sergeant Fang Mulheisen. Author Jackson knows the ethnic and racial boundaries that divide Detroit, and he has a feel for the neighborhood bars and gathering places. The police details all ring true, and Mulheisen is a suitably cynical cop. Mob bosses are being killed, and no one is certain who is behind it in this series entry.

Mosley, Walter

Devil in a Blue Dress. **Easy Rawlins mysteries.** 1990. W. W. Norton, ISBN 0393028542, 219p.

In Mosley's books, as in Raymond Chandler's, the city of Los Angeles is central to the story. It is hard to imagine these tales set anywhere else. But Mosley expands on the theme, capturing both the white and the black communities in LA, and brings them to life. The series covers the 1940s (the setting for this title) through the 1960s, and Mosley creates an eloquent portrait of the changes in LA in the postwar years. Here, his protagonist Easy Rawlins finds work as an investigator after losing his factory job and is hired to track down a missing white woman.

O'Brien, Martin

Jacquot and the Waterman. **Inspector Jacquot mysteries.** 2006. St. Martin's Minotaur, ISBN 031234998X, 416p.

The port city of Marseilles has a seamy reputation as an entrepôt for black-market goods and gunrunning. Like most big cities, it finds well-to-do communities rubbing up against blighted neighborhoods, and crime often links the two. Inspector Daniel Jacquot knows the dark side of the city, and Marseilles becomes almost a character in the story. The inspector is on the hunt for a serial killer in this series debut.

Pelecanos, George

Down By the River Where the Dead Men Go. **Nick Stefanos mysteries.** 1999. Serpent's Tail, ISBN 1852427167, 240p.

Visitors to Washington, DC, take in the Capitol, the White House, and other monuments of civic life. Fortunately for most of them, they never see the streets that Pelacanos covers in his bleak and moody series. Pelacanos knows the intimate details of life in DC, and his knowledge adds to the realism of these violent and despairing tales that feature an alcoholic PI, Nick Stefanos.

Here, Stefanos awakens from a drunk and hears a murder committed and steps into the investigation.

Out on the Rural Route: Crime in the Country

Sometimes, you are looking for a crime fiction story that takes you out of the big, bad city and centers on misdoings in the countryside. It is assumed that rural life is more peaceful and bucolic, but as the authors listed here demonstrate, the crimes and misdemeanors that take place outside of town are as varied, and can be as horrifying, as those in the more typical urban settings. Small towns and isolated homesteads can have just as much to hide as a San Francisco apartment complex or a New York brownstone.

Crider, Bill
Ghost of a Chance. **Sheriff Dan Rhodes mysteries.** 2001. Worldwide Library, ISBN 0373263961, 256p.

> Crider's series featuring Sheriff Dan Rhodes is set in remote Blacklin County, Texas. Crider has a great sense of life in a rural Texas town, and the books feature a blend of folksy humor and small-town goings-on. Despite the small size of the town, the sheriff has plenty of work to keep him busy and a host of eccentric characters to ride herd on. Here, a series of ghostly visitations is followed by murder, and Rhodes has his hands full.

D'Amato, Barbara
A Hard Christmas. **Cat Marsala mysteries.** 1996. Berkley, ISBN 0425154653, 288p.

> Investigative reporter Cat Marsala is more commonly found prowling the streets of Chicago looking for a story and uncovering murder. But a story on Christmas tree farming takes Cat up to rural Michigan to visit a family tree farm. Instead of an idyllic portrait of rural felicity, Cat uncovers a tangled web of secrets that lead to murder. D'Amato astutely manages the transition from city to countryside and includes interesting details on the tree farming business.

Hills, Kathleen
Past Imperfect. **John McIntyre mysteries.** 2003. Worldwide Library, ISBN 0373264712, 304p.

> Michigan's Upper Peninsula, and the families who farm the land there, are the focus of Hills's series. John McIntyre grew up in this community but left to work in military intelligence. On his return, he took a position as constable of Saint Adele Township, assuming that he would have little to deal with beyond the normal misdemeanors of a small community. Much of the pleasure here

comes from the contrast between McIntyre's memories of the community as a child and the realities of life there in the present day.

McCrumb, Sharon

⇨ *The Ballad of Frankie Silver.* **Ballad mysteries.** 1999. Signet, ISBN 0451197399, 416p.

Rural Appalachia is the setting for the stories in McCrumb's Ballad series, and she writes descriptively and eloquently about the land and the people who inhabit it. In many of the stories, McCrumb reflects on the links between the past and the present, as here, in which Sheriff Spencer Arrowood is forced to rethink the arrest of a man years earlier who is now awaiting execution. Arrowood ponders the case in light of an old story about another wrongful execution.

Oleksiw, Susan

A *Murderous Innocence.* **Mellingham mysteries.** 2006. Five Star, ISBN 1594143757, 263p.

If you take Norman Rockwell paintings at face value, New England village life can seem quite idyllic. Oleksiw understands the appeal of this view and captures many of the positive aspects of life in a small Massachusetts village. But below the surface, tensions and grudges exist that rival those between any urban street gangs. Mellingham's police chief, Joe Silva, here investigates drug abuse in the town, punctuated by murder.

Penny, Louise

Still Life. 2006. St. Martin's Minotaur, ISBN 0312352557, 320p.

The small Canadian village of Three Pines is the setting for Penny's debut mystery. As in other small-town crime fiction, the serene nature of the community is shattered by a murder, in this case of a retired teacher. When outside investigators arrive from the Quebec Sûreté, they discover that the town holds a variety of secrets that could be behind the death. Penny writes lyrically of rural Canada and the people there.

Sultry Crimes: Hot, Steamy Mystery Locales

A hot, sticky, sweltering heat pervades all of the stories on this list. When the temperatures and the humidity rise, tempers get short, and reasonable people find themselves doing unreasonable things. What might seem like a momentary slight suddenly demands a response, and before you know it, there's a body on the floor. The titles here will warm up the coldest day and leave you sweating and eager for a cool breeze.

Carver, Caroline
Dead Heat. 2004. Mysterious Press, ISBN 0892967781, 336p.

A career in publishing was Georgia Parish's ticket out of the heat and humidity of northern Australia. When she returns home for a funeral, her desire is to escape the heat and the jungle as quickly as possible. But a sabotaged plane flight that nearly kills her and does kill two others leads Parish into a spiral of danger and death in the steamy Queensland heat.

Cleverly, Barbara
Palace Tiger. **Detective Joe Sandilands mysteries.** 2005. Carroll and Graf, ISBN 0786715723, 304p.

The Raj is nearing an end as Scotland Yard Detective Joe Sandilands solves crimes in British India. Cleverly understands both the English and Indian cultures and writes compellingly of their intersection. Here, Sandilands finds himself investigating the suspicious deaths of the heirs to a maharajate. The steamy heat of India comes through in Cleverly's descriptions.

Garcia-Aguilera, Carolina
Havana Heat. **Lupe Solano mysteries.** 2001. Avon, ISBN 0380807386, 352p.

Lupe Solano is a tough PI working in the heart of Miami's Cuban exile community. Passions run as hot as the temperatures here, especially when Castro's Cuba is recalled. Lupe's search for a hidden medieval tapestry takes her from Miami to the sweltering Cuban capitol, Havana. Hot art, hot temperatures, and hot feelings make this a memorable title.

Garcia-Roza, Luiz Alfredo
⇨ *Window in Copacabana*. **Inspector Espinosa mysteries.** 2006. Picador, ISBN 031242566X, 256p.

You can feel the heat on every page of this series set in Rio de Janeiro, Brazil. Inspector Espinosa is investigating a string of cop killings, and the temperatures in Rio are topping at 100 degrees or more. Corruption is at the heart of the mystery here. Garcia-Roza is a Brazilian mystery writer whose police procedurals shine for their characters, their noirish feel, and their steamy setting.

Jordan, River
The Gin Girl. 2003. Livingston Press, ISBN 1931982171, 258p.

It gets sticky in the swamps of the Gulf Coast islands, and Jordan's tale of a hard-drinking girl who comes back to her home is steeped in the humidity and heat of the Florida coast. Mary returns to her home on Toliquilah and tries to track down her former sweetheart, who has disappeared, but no one can say to where. As she begins to ask questions, the temperatures and the dangers rise in this lyrical and thoughtful story.

Padura, Leonardo
Havana Red. **Mario Conde mysteries.** 2005. Bitter Lemon Press, ISBN 1904738095, 233p.

    The climate can be as oppressive as the Castro regime in contemporary Cuba. Padura, a native of the island, captures the nature of both in his series featuring Inspector Mario Conde. The inspector investigates the murder of a transvestite, who happens to be the son of a government official. Padura writes about contemporary life in Havana in a loving, but clear-eyed style, and the city and its people come to life.

Smith, Julie
House of Blues. **Skip Langdon mysteries.** 1996. Fawcett, ISBN 0804113424, 352p.

    As a character remarks in one of Smith's Skip Langdon mysteries, the heat changes the brain chemistry, releasing people from their inhibitions. If that is the case, that would account for the variety of troubles that New Orleans cop Langdon encounters on her watch. Smith has a feel for the steamy feel of the Big Easy, and in this tale of the murder of a family patriarch the city itself is an important character.

The Valley of Dry Bones: Crime in Arid Lands

    Hot, dry winds and scorching sun, vultures circling, and nothing moving but a lizard or two are the features of the mysteries on this list. Although the settings may range from the arroyos and canyons of the U.S. Southwest to the African savannahs to the sandy deserts of North Africa, you can feel the heat in each of the stories listed here. These arid lands are perilous by nature and are even more so when the human element arrives.

Anaya, Rudolfo
Zia Summer. **Sonny Baca mysteries.** 1996. Warner Books, ISBN 0446603163, 368p.

    The culture of the Southwest, particularly the Hispanic community, is at the heart of Anaya's mysteries. The people, their traditions, and, most important, the landscape all come under Anaya's view, which is as remorseless as the New Mexican sun. Here, Sonny Baca investigates the murder of his cousin, and finds politics and environmental issues impeding his investigation.

Burns, Rex
The Leaning Land. **Gabe Wager mysteries.** 1997. Walker, ISBN 0802733069, 269p.

    Taking the detective out of his normal setting offers an author interesting opportunities for character development. Here, Denver police detective Gabe

Wager must head out to western Colorado, a land of harsh skies and desert, to work with federal agents on a series of violent attacks on the Squaw Point Reservation. Wager is caught between sides—the feds, the tribal police, local landowners, and a militia group—and the barren ground does not offer much relief.

Hillerman, Tony

Thief of Time. **Joe Leaphorn and Jim Chee mysteries.** 1990. HarperTorch, ISBN 0061000043, 352p.

Hillerman is the acknowledged king of U.S. Southwest crime fiction. His Leaphorn and Chee mysteries all feature a strong sense of the rhythms and seasons of Arizona and New Mexico. The detectives are as relentless as the scorching sun, and Hillerman's depictions of the land always ring true. Here, the investigation centers on pillaging of Native American sites and associated murders.

Jance, J. A.

Skeleton Canyon. **Joanna Brady mysteries.** 2004. Avon, ISBN 0380724332, 400p.

Sheriff Joanna Brady keeps the peace in Cochise County, Arizona. Things are hot there, and it is not just the temperature. Out on the Mexico–United States border, tempers can run high, and Sheriff Brady is looking for a missing Anglo teenager whose boyfriend is of Mexican descent. Her parents have no doubt that he is responsible for her disappearance, but Sheriff Brady is not so sure. The stark, lovely Arizona environment contrasts with the violence of the crimes, and the heat of the Arizona summer glances off every page.

McCall Smith, Alexander

The No. 1 Ladies Detective Agency. **Precious Ramotswe mysteries.** 2002. Anchor, ISBN 1400031346, 240p.

In Botswana, on the edge of the Kalahari Desert, it is dry and dusty. McCall Smith makes the people and the land come alive through his descriptions and understanding of the culture. Precious Ramotswe has sold her late father's cattle and set up a detective agency in Gaborone. McCall Smith's passion for Africa resonates throughout the stories, and Ramotswe's wit and power of observation make her a delightful detective.

Pearce, Michael

⇨ *The Mamur Zapt and the Return of the Carpet*. **Mamur Zapt mysteries.** 2006. Poisoned Pen Press, ISBN 1890208779, 252p.

Egypt prior to World War I was an uneasy country, under British occupation, and chafing at British rule. The Mamur Zapt headed the political investigation unit in Cairo, and in this series is a Welshman. Although the mysteries are elegant and intriguing, these books are equally interesting for Pearce's affectionate and atmospheric descriptions of Cairo and its environs. Dust and bright light seem to pervade the series.

Talton, John
Arizona Dreams. **David Mapstone mysteries.** 2006. Poisoned Pen Press, ISBN 1590583183, 216p.

Water is essential to life, and that is especially true in the desert environment of the U.S. Southwest. David Mapstone and his wife, both deputies in Phoenix, investigate a series of killings in the desert that appear to be related to a new development planned on land that needs water. Native Arizonan Talton's descriptions of the relentlessness of the heat of an Arizona summer are spot-on. The pages shimmer and you can almost see the mirages.

Cold as Death: Crime Fiction that Chills

As Robert Frost noted, the world could end in either fire or ice. In the titles on this list, the authors have all chosen the latter, setting their stories in the frozen Northern Hemisphere. Although passions may burn hot here, the settings will chill you to the bone, and there is nothing as cold as death.

Doogan, Mike
Lost Angel. 2006. Putnam, ISBN 0399153713, 304p.

Nik Kane is a former Alaskan police detective who is just out of prison after being framed. A Christian community in the remote Alaskan interior calls on Kane to investigate the disappearance of a teenage girl. The cold seeps off the pages of Doogan's debut novel. His descriptions of the cutting cold of the Alaskan winter will thoroughly chill you, as will the mystery.

Henry, Sue
Murder on the Yukon Quest. **Jessie Arnold and Alex Jensen mysteries.** 2000. Avon, ISBN 0380788640, 320p.

Everyone knows the Iditarod sled dog race, but the Yukon Quest, a 1,000-mile race between Fairbanks, Alaska, and Whitehorse, Yukon Territory, is equally, if not more, demanding. Henry's mystery follows the race and a trail of murder and abduction. The biggest enemy here is the harsh Yukon winter, which is chillingly described. Henry draws a portrait of a beautiful land that is also unforgivingly dangerous.

Hoeg, Peter
Smilla's Sense of Snow. 1994. Island Books, ISBN 0440218535, 499p.

A native of Greenland, Smilla Jasperson lives in Copenhagen, Denmark, and she has studied the science of snow and ice. When the young son of a neighboring family falls to his death from an icy roof, Smilla suspects from the patterns in the snow that this was not an accident, and she feels compelled to investigate. The constant references to physical cold and ice reflect Smilla's cold and rather lonely existence. Hoeg's book is like an ice palace: beautiful and chilling.

Larsson, Asa

Sun Storm. **Rebecka Martinsson mysteries.** 2006. Delacorte, ISBN 038533981X, 320p.

Northern Sweden's arctic territory is the setting for Larsson's series debut. Attorney Rebecka Martinsson is called home to the remote north of Sweden to investigate the killing of the leader of a fundamentalist church that she had been part of. Larsson's descriptions of the play of light on the winter's snow and ice and of the aurora borealis are as breathtaking as a winter blast.

Smith, Martin Cruz

Gorky Park. **Arkady Renko mysteries.** 1999. Pan, ISBN 033026673X, 336p.

Smith's first mystery featuring Russian homicide detective Arkady Renko begins in a most chilling fashion. Three bodies are discovered in a Moscow park, frozen and mutilated. Renko's investigation leads him to a cold-blooded mix of political and business corruption and to trouble with the KGB and the FBI. Renko's Russian fatalism is mirrored in the cold and dreary Moscow settings.

Spencer-Fleming, Julia

In the Bleak Midwinter. **Reverend Clare Fergusson mysteries.** 2003. St. Martin's Minotaur, ISBN 0312986769, 384p.

Reverend Clare Fergusson is the new priest of the Episcopal church in a small town in Upstate New York. The town is unsure what to do with a "lady priest," and her reception seems as cold as the winter weather. Then a newborn baby is left on the rectory doorstep, and shortly afterward the mother, a local teen, is found dead. The reverend joins forces with the local police chief to track down the killer. The biting cold of a New York winter is present throughout the story.

Stabenow, Dana

Fine and Bitter Snow. **Kate Shugak mysteries.** 2003. St. Martin's Minotaur, ISBN 0312989474, 320p.

Stabenow's mysteries are set in Alaska and feature attorney and PI Kate Shugak. This series entry centers on oil drilling in an Alaskan wilderness area, where Kate grew up, and pits conservationists against corporations. Stabenow writes elegantly of the beauty and the danger of the Alaskan wilderness, especially when winter has set in, and Kate is a competent and capable detective who teams up with state trooper Jim Chopin to solve a series of killings related to the controversy.

The Heights of Murder: Mountaintop Mysteries

Crime fiction authors frequently use beautiful settings to provide a contrast with the sordid goings-on in the story. At the same time, placing a mystery in a mountainous setting adds an extra layer of physical danger to the story. The stories on this list all take advantage of one or both of these options. These high-altitude mysteries will leave you breathless in more ways than one.

Eslick, Tom
Mountain Peril. **White Mountains mysteries.** 2005. Viking, ISBN 0670033863, 288p.

    Eslick's sleuth, Will Buchanan, is a high school teacher and part of a search-and-rescue team that works in New Hampshire's White Mountains. Eslick's knowledge of high-altitude search and rescue, and his lyrical writing about the landscape, add to the appeal of the stories. In this entry in the series, Buchanan stumbles across a body while on a search mission, but it is not the person the team is looking for. It seems a serial killer is planting corpses along the trail.

Johnson, Craig
The Cold Dish. **Walt Longmire mysteries.** 2004. Viking, ISBN 0670033693, 384p.

    The high country of Wyoming is the setting for Johnson's western procedurals featuring Sheriff Walt Longmire. Johnson deftly paints a picture of the spaciousness, the breathtaking beauty, and the danger of the Wyoming mountains. The landscape frequently shapes the lives of the characters and the mystery. Here, a teenage boy, one of four boys who was convicted of rape and received a suspended sentence, is killed. It's an exciting and violent tale of revenge in a majestic setting.

Maron, Margaret
High Country Fall. **Deborah Knott mysteries.** 2005. Warner, ISBN 0446615900, 320p.

    The chance to fill in for a vacationing judge takes Judge Deborah Knott into the Blue Ridge Mountains. She is seeking some peace and quiet and the opportunity to enjoy the coming of autumn. Things are not as peaceful as they seem, though, and the town is split over plans to develop the mountain. The beautiful fall scenery provides a stark contrast to the murders that Judge Knott must unravel.

McKinzie, Clinton
⇨ *The Edge of Justice.* **Antonio Burns mysteries.** 2003. Dell, ISBN 0440237238, 448p.

    Special Agent Antonio Burns works for the Wyoming Department of Criminal Investigation and is a passionate climber (as is author McKinzie). The excitement here comes both from the mystery, in which Burns investigates the apparently accidental death of a climber, and from McKinzie's skill at capturing the exhilaration and the danger of mountain climbing. This series is high-altitude crime fiction at its best.

McManus, Patrick

Avalanche. **Bo Tully mysteries.** 2007. Simon and Schuster, ISBN 141653265X, 304p.

Noted outdoor humorist McManus turns his hand to crime fiction in this witty series set in fictional Blight County, Idaho. Sheriff Bo Tully's job is usually pretty peaceful, and when a resort lodge owner goes missing, Tully looks on it as an opportunity to get into the mountains. An avalanche traps Tully and the lodge guests, though, and the missing owner turns up dead. McManus offers up an enjoyable mix of humor and high-country scenery.

Pattison, Eliot

Bone Mountain. **Shan Tao Yun mysteries.** 2004. St. Martin's Griffin, ISBN 0312330898, 432p.

You cannot get much higher than the Himalayas, the chilling setting for Pattison's brooding series featuring former Chinese prosecutor Shan Tao Yun. Shan was demoted and sent to prison in remote Tibet but has been released and has agreed to help return a sacred relic to its home in a Tibetan village. Murder ensues, but the story is equally gripping for its descriptions of the Tibetan mountains and their people.

Sprague, Gretchen

Death by Thunder. 2005. St. Martin's Minotaur, ISBN 0312347677, 288p.

The hills of the Hudson Valley are a far cry from those of Tibet or the Rocky Mountains, but Sprague captures them in their beauty and danger. Two seemingly accidental falls from the cliffs are at the heart of the mystery, and art gallery owner Janet Upton is an able investigator. The crimes seem to tie into a clash between preserving the mountains and developing them, and Upton's uncle, a council member, dies right before a crucial vote.

Schooled in Death: Murder in the Academic World

If the cloister and monastery seem unusual locales for crime and detection, then the halls of academe might seem equally peaceful to those who are outside of them. But mystery writers understand that the jealousies and competition between scholars can be cutthroat, at times literally so. Here are some of the best of the academic mysteries, ranging from the cozy to the dark, but all portray some of the elements of the world of intellectual endeavor and learning for its own sake.

Borthwick, J. S.
Coup de Grace. **Sarah Deane mysteries.** 2001. St. Martin's Press, ISBN 0312974493, 221p.

With her new PhD in hand, English scholar and amateur detective Sarah Deane heads off to fill a temporary position at a prestigious boarding school for girls in Massachusetts. Boarding schools are notorious for eccentric faculty, and Merritt is no exception. The faculty includes French instructor Madame Carpentier, who is known as a terror of the student body. When another teacher is killed while wearing Madame Carpentier's distinctive cape, Sarah Deane must step in and uncover the killer. Borthwick captures the characters of both faculty and students in this delightful tale.

Bowen, Gail
A Killing Spring. **Joanne Kilbourn mysteries.** 1997. McClelland and Stewart, ISBN 0771014864, 272p.

In this entry in her Joanne Kilbourn series, Bowen explores the academic rivalries that can lead to more than just an outburst at a department meeting and hurt feelings. Kilbourn, a university professor in Saskatchewan, is drawn into the investigation of the death of a fellow professor, whose body is found in an unseemly situation. Suicide seems likely, but Kilbourn is uncertain, especially after other events on campus appear to be connected. Bowen has a fine sense for the interactions between professors and students.

Crider, Bill
Murder Is an Art. **Professor Sally Good mysteries.** 1999. Thomas Dunne Books, ISBN 0312199279, 243p.

Crider is known as much for his humor as for his mysteries, and here he provides ample evidence of each. English professor Sally Good feels that the pace of the investigation into the murder of a colleague in the art department at Hughes Community College is moving too slowly, and she steps in to solve the crime. Crider understands the faculty lounge as well as the crafting of a pleasant mystery.

Morson, Ian
Falconer's Crusade. **William Falconer mysteries.** 1997. St. Martin's Press, ISBN 0312956975, 220p.

Academic crime is not limited to the contemporary campus. Morson's series is set on the grounds of Oxford University in the thirteenth century. Featuring scholar and instructor William Falconer, the books combine a fascinating portrait of medieval scholarship with a cunning plot. The murders of a townsperson and several Oxford students take Falconer away from his studies to protect one of his students who is accused of the crimes. Morson's books have a darker tone than many academic mysteries.

Poulson, Christine

Murder Is Academic. **Cambridge mysteries.** 2004. St. Martin's Press, ISBN 0312318073, 240p.

With its Cambridge University setting, it would be easy to assume that this is another English cozy mystery with eccentric dons and lively students. Poulson, however, is as interested in the lives of her characters and their individual stories as in the solution of the crime. That's not to say that she slights the academic side of the story, though. Professor Cassandra James comes to teach English at a fictional college at Cambridge University and finds herself taking on the role of department head after the accidental death of the current chair. In cleaning out papers, though, James discovers that the death was more likely murder.

Raphael, Lev

Burning Down the House. **Nick Hoffman mysteries.** 2001. Walker, ISBN 0802733654, 256p.

Readers looking for a darker and more suspenseful story set in the groves of academe should try Raphael's Nick Hoffman series. Openly gay, Hoffman teaches at a fictional state university in Michigan that seems to be the last stop on the academic train, and Raphael is unsparing in his portrayal of the pettiness of college politics. Departmental jealousies erupt in harassment of a professor, and when Hoffman investigates, he discovers that they can also lead to violence. The suspense carries the reader along.

Sayers, Dorothy

⇨ *Gaudy Night.* **Lord Peter Wimsey mysteries.** 1995. Harper Torch, ISBN 0061043494, 512p.

Sayers's story explores the world of scholarship for its own sake and looks at the conflict between a life of thinking and a life of doing. Set in a fictional women's college attached to Oxford University, *Gaudy Night* features Harriet Vane, alumna of the college, now seeking respite from the world. She returns to investigate a series of poison-pen letters that have been circulating to faculty and students, and her presence on the grounds leads to more disturbances. The tale is also notable in that in it Sayers resolves the romance between Harriet and Lord Peter Wimsey, who arrives to assist Harriet in her investigations.

Chapter Four

Mood

Mood may be one of the most difficult appeal characteristics to fully capture. In part, this is because the mood a book creates involves both the intentions and craft of the writer and the expectations and responses of the reader to the writer's work. Language, pacing, story, and characters can all affect the mood that emanates from a particular book. At the same time, readers bring their own feelings to the book, and this determines, to a great extent, their perception of the work's mood. No two readers will respond the same way to a particular title, and the titles in this list offer something for readers who are in a wide range of moods.

Also listed here are those titles that are bending the definition of genre. Cross-genre writing is a growing trend, and many writers are crafting works of crime fiction that incorporate ideas and themes from fantasy, horror, science fiction, romance, and other genres. These books can often serve as good introductions to the crime and mystery genre for readers who do not normally read in this area.

The lists here focus on the ways the books feel to the reader and on the reactions that a reader might have to the specific titles listed.

The Golden Age

The period from the 1920s to the 1950s is often referred to as the golden age of English mystery writing. This period saw a flourishing of well-written, popular crime novels, and a number of these golden age authors are widely read even today. These stories almost always center on the puzzle, they usually feature an amateur detective, and they are filled with red herrings that may lead the reader astray. Nonetheless, most of these authors follow the "rules of fair play," laid out by Father Ronald Knox (for a discussion of fair play and Knox, see the introduction), and the author provides all the clues necessary for the reader to solve the mystery along with the detective. These titles generally keep the depictions of violence and sex to a minimum, and in almost all cases justice is triumphant.

Allingham, Marjorie

Death of a Ghost. **Albert Campion mysteries.** 1997. Carroll and Graf, ISBN 0786704411, 192p.

> Albert Campion, Allingham's sleuth, is suave and sophisticated, as are many golden age detectives. He is in the line of aristocratic crime solvers, whose social standing allows them access to high society and all of its crimes. The Campion stories are witty and elegantly written. They always have a well-crafted puzzle and are filled with interesting characters. Here, Campion investigates murder in the art world.

Carr, John Dickson

Case of the Constant Suicides. **Gideon Fell mysteries.** 2002. Black Dagger Crime, ISBN 0754086151, 168p.

> Carr is a master of the locked room mystery, a staple of the golden age. The body is found in a room, locked from the inside, with no sign of forced entry. The reader and the detective must puzzle out how the crime was committed. Carr's Gideon Fell is a corpulent, beer-drinking historian who never bends his knee for a clue, but he is a master at using logic to tie together seemingly unrelated evidence. This case involves three deaths that could be suicides or murders.

Christie, Agatha

⇨ *The Mysterious Affair at Styles*. **Hercule Poirot mysteries.** 2002. Wildside Press, ISBN 1592248888, 188p.

> Christie is the queen of the golden age, known for her elaborate plots full of misdirection. *The Mysterious Affair at Styles* introduced readers to that master of ratiocination, Belgian detective Hercule Poirot. Poirot is a dandy, vain of his appearance, and supremely confident in his abilities, and it is rare that his "little grey cells" let him down. Poirot's first case involves the death of a wealthy woman, whose children, servants, and new husband all may have had reason to kill her. Poirot is called in to the case by his future sidekick, Captain Hastings, who is a friend of the family.

Marsh, Ngaio

A Man Lay Dead. **Inspector Alleyn mysteries.** 1997. St. Martin's, ISBN 0312963580, 192p.

> Marsh differs from her golden age companions in that her sleuth is a police inspector rather than an amateur detective. But with her clever puzzles,

interesting settings, and satisfying conclusions, Marsh's Roderick Alleyn stories fit right in with the best of the golden age. This first in the series brings Alleyn to an English manor house to solve a murder.

Queen, Ellery
The Egyptian Cross Mystery. **Ellery Queen mysteries.** 1971. Gollancz, ISBN 0575006161, 318p.

Crime fiction writer Ellery Queen (actually two cousins writing together) gave a U.S. touch to the golden age mystery. Queen's work shares all the elements of the best British golden age crime novels: humor, a classic puzzle, and an amusing, intelligent, and witty sleuth. Narrated by Queen, who is also the detective here, *The Egyptian Cross Mystery* takes the reader from West Virginia to New England to solve a killing seemingly rooted in a feud that began in the Balkans.

Sayers, Dorothy
Strong Poison. **Lord Peter Wimsey mysteries.** 1995. HarperTorch, ISBN 0061043508, 272p.

Sayers is considered by many to be the greatest of the golden age crime novelists. She blends a fascinating puzzle with believable characters that grow from book to book. Sayers writes eloquently of the human condition in all its grandeur and weakness. *Strong Poison* introduces Harriet Vane, on trial for her life after being accused of murdering her lover. The defense brings Lord Peter Wimsey into the case to investigate the accusation. Sayers explores the relationship between Harriet and Lord Peter through the rest of the novels in the series.

Stout, Rex
Black Orchids. **Nero Wolfe mysteries.** 1992. Crimeline, ISBN 0553257196, 208p.

Like Ellery Queen, Rex Stout is a U.S. crime writer who captures the sensibility of the golden age. The settings shift from the manor houses and villages of England to the brownstones of New York City. Wolfe epitomizes the intellectual genius detective who makes connections between the clues to solve the case. Here, an orchid show lures Wolfe out of his home, and when a murder occurs at the show, Wolfe and his partner, Archie Goodwin, are called on to investigate.

Tey, Josephine
Daughter of Time. **Alan Grant mysteries.** 1988. Scribner Paper, ISBN 0020545509, 208p.

Tey's mysteries are often rooted in scholarship, and she may be best known for *Daughter of Time*. English Police Inspector Alan Grant is recuperating in a hospital and is driven to distraction by boredom. A friend brings him a book of historical portraits, and Grant is drawn to the portrait of Richard III. He proceeds to explore, from his hospital bed, the case against Richard for murdering his nephews, the princes in the Tower. Tey's reconstruction of the historical evidence is masterful.

Ain't Got No Body:
Cozy Mysteries

Many of the golden age crime fiction writers were masters of the cozy mystery. Cozies have remained popular ever since, and, for many mystery readers, the cozy mystery meets all their needs. In a cozy mystery, most of the deaths occur offstage, and even when death makes a visit there is a distinct lack of violence. The same applies to sex. Romance is a frequent component in cozies, but things tend to remain relatively chaste. Although the action may be mellow, the characters and the humor in cozies keep the reader entertained and coming back for more. So for readers who are looking for a clever story with a well-crafted puzzle that is neither gory nor steamy, here is a list of some of the best contemporary cozy mysteries.

Atherton, Nancy
Aunt Dimity's Good Deed. **Aunt Dimity mysteries.** 1998. Penguin, ISBN 0140258817, 288p.
　　Atherton's Aunt Dimity books blend together a beguiling concoction of mystery and ghost story and at the same time offer an appealing cast of characters. In this third book in the series, ghostly Aunt Dimity and her earthly helper, Lori Shepherd are on the hunt to track down Lori's missing father-in-law. Atherton presents an interesting twist on the traditional cozy.

Beaton, M. C.
Death of a Poison Pen. **Hamish MacBeth mysteries.** 2005. Warner Books, ISBN 0446614890, 256p.
　　A recent addition in the Hamish MacBeth series, *Death of a Poison Pen* exemplifies Beaton's deft handling of romance, mystery, humor, and eccentric characters. Beaton's books offer an enchanting portrait of village life in rural Scotland as well as a finely plotted mystery. Here, a series of poison-pen letters leads to murder and suicide, and it is up to police constable Hamish MacBeth to sort out the problem.

Bowen, Rhys
⇨ *Evans Above*. **Evan Evans mysteries.** 1998. Berkley, ISBN 0425166422, 224p.
　　With an interesting setting in the Welsh countryside and an appealing cast of characters, Bowen's series will interest most fans of the cozy genre. The eponymous Evans is a young police constable in a small village in Wales. In

this introductory story, Evans is called on to solve the deaths of two hikers, who apparently fell in separate accidents. Bowen mixes humor and a strong sense of place in her mysteries.

Hart, Carolyn G.
Murder Walks the Plank. **Annie Laurance Darling mysteries.** 2005. Avon, ISBN 0060004754, 336p.

South Carolina mystery bookstore owner Annie Laurance Darling is known for her love of mystery fiction and her mystery painting contests, held at the store. When a murder mystery cruise that she is running is interrupted by the death of one of the participants, Annie and her husband, Max, investigate. Hart includes lots of references to other crime fiction in her fast-paced and well-plotted cozies.

Hess, Joan
Malpractice in Maggody. **Arly Hanks mysteries.** 2006. Pocket, ISBN 074344390X. 384p.

Hess's series is set in a small town in the Ozarks and features a plethora of unpredictable characters and a clever and sassy female police chief. Readers will enjoy the small-town setting and Hess's ear for humorous dialogue. In this entry in the series, a secretive rehab clinic for the semifamous has ousted the residents of the retirement home. The townsfolk of Maggody want to know more about the place. When a series of murders occurs at the facility police Chief Arly Hanks steps in.

MacPherson, Rett
Blood Relations. **Torie O'Shea mysteries.** 2003. St. Martin's Minotaur, ISBN 0312301715, 288p.

The quintessential cozy detective is often the village snoop, and who does more nosing about in local history than a genealogist? MacPherson's Torie O'Shea is a mother and avid local historian who turns up bodies as often as she finds third cousins. The unearthing of a sunken riverboat, the death of one of the discoverers, and the simultaneous discovery of an unsuspected half sister give O'Shea ample areas for her investigations.

Page, Katherine Hall
The Body in the Bog. **Faith Fairchild mysteries.** 1997. Avon, ISBN 0380727129, 384p.

In the small Massachusetts community of Aleford, Faith Fairchild is married to a minister, raising a family, and running a catering business. But she also finds time to investigate local mysteries. An excellent read for fans of the cozy mystery in a present-day setting, Page's series is strong on the details of village life, and includes several New England recipes. Here, possible development of a natural area leads to violence and murder.

Purser, Ann
Fear on Friday. **Lois Meade mysteries.** 2006. Berkley, ISBN 0425212254, 272p.

Often, the village sleuth is a nosy old woman peering out of her windows who cannot keep out of her neighbors' business. Purser turns that theme on its head with Lois Meade, a house cleaner by trade who gets invited into people's houses. And what better disguise for an amateur detective than a house cleaner? You get to pry into the corners and get paid for it. In this series entry, Lois has expanded her cleaning business to the next town over and discovers that more needs cleaning than the windows. Purser has a good feel for English village life.

Bloody Murder: The Goriest Crime Fiction

At the opposite end of the crime fiction scale from the cozies are those stories whose violence level and body count are all too realistically high. The story can be a fast-paced thriller with lots of action or may as commonly be a meditative exploration of the impact of violence on the human condition (think of a Sergio Leone or Akira Kurosawa film). In either case, though, the body counts are high, and it is often the detective who contributes to the mayhem. Readers looking for violent crimes and violent retribution will find enjoyment here.

Block, Lawrence
⇨ *Ticket to the Boneyard*. **Matthew Scudder mysteries.** 1991. Avon, ISBN 0380709945, 384p.

Block's Matthew Scudder is a deeply flawed man. An alcoholic ex-cop, Scudder works as a private eye in New York. In his past, Scudder framed a man who richly deserved jail, but now the ex-con is out and seeking revenge on Scudder, others who helped put him away, and anyone else who stands in the way. The violence and fear are realistically portrayed in Block's chilling story.

Box, C. J.
In Plain Sight. **Joe Pickett mysteries.** 2006. Putnam, ISBN 0399153608, 320p.

Revenge brings out the worst in people. Wyoming Game Warden Joe Pickett is being stalked by a killer bent on avenging the death of his sister-in-law and her family, which he blames on Pickett. The killer leaves a trail of bodies in his wake. To make matters more difficult, Pickett finds himself embroiled in a family feud after the matriarch of a wealthy ranch family apparently dies.

Ellroy, James
Blood on the Moon. **L.A. Noir trilogy.** 2005. Vintage, ISBN 140009528X, 272p.

Readers come to Elroy for his dark, literary crime writing, set in Los Angeles. In *Blood on the Moon,* Elroy brings together a serial killer and the cop responsible for tracking him down and compares and contrasts their lives and motives. Not for the squeamish, this is a blood-haunted story, and the protagonist is almost as disturbing as the killer.

Hunsicker, Harry
Still River. **Lee Henry Oswald mysteries.** 2006. St. Martin's Minotaur, ISBN 0312940904, 304p.

The seamy side of Dallas is the setting for Hunsicker's noir thrillers. His protagonist, wisecracking PI Lee Henry Oswald, faces drug gangs, real estate barons, and a host of other villains in this debut outing. The violence is visceral, sometimes literally. Oswald has a fascinating assortment of scary sidekicks who make it occasionally difficult to tell the good guys from the bad.

O'Connell, Carol
Killing Critics. **Kathleen Mallory mysteries.** 1997. Jove, ISBN 0515120863, 400p.

NYPD Officer Kathleen Mallory is almost as disturbing as the criminals she pursues. Mallory is cold, brilliant, and prone to violence, and O'Connell does not shy away from the gritty details of urban police work. The gruesome death of an art critic leads Mallory back to an earlier case that baffled her adoptive detective father. The crimes are chilling in their violence, and Mallory is equally cold in her dispensing of justice.

Pelecanos, George
Soul Circus. **Derek Strange and Terry Quinn mysteries.** 2004. Warner Vision, ISBN 0446611425, 416p.

Pelecanos is known for his relentless portrayal of crime and justice in Washington, DC. Here, Pelecanos explores how the mixture of easy access to drugs and guns has torn apart the lives of individuals and of the community. His private eyes, Strange and Quinn, are caught up in the violent world of drug gangs as they are hired by the defense team in a capital murder case.

Wilson, Robert
The Big Killing. **Bruce Medway mysteries.** 2003. Harvest Books, ISBN 0156011190, 336p.

The west coast of Africa is a violent and dangerous place. The breakdown of civil order in Liberia is spilling over to the Ivory Coast, where expat Englishman Bruce Medway provides services for those who can pay. Explicit violence, backed by corruption and greed, is a staple of Wilson's Medway novels, and *The Big Killing* is true to form. Wilson's strong sense of place adds to the appeal.

Love and Death: Crimes of Passion

Love may be the biggest mystery of all, and crimes of passion are a staple of mystery fiction. Affairs end badly, someone gets upset, and the next thing you know there's a body on the floor and the police are on the way. But love and all its messy tangles also can be found in other places in crime novels. It may be the romantic difficulties of the detective or a torrid night of passion between to lonely people. These encounters make the characters more human and sometimes spice up the story quite a bit. The titles listed here all explore the more lusty sides of detection.

Bartholomew, Nancy

Film Strip. **Sierra Lavotini mysteries.** 2001. St. Martin's Minotaur, ISBN 0312977441, 288p.

Bartholomew's series featuring stripper Sierra Lavotini will definitely steam up your glasses. Lavotini is a statuesque blonde who makes no excuses for her line of work but rather revels in it. In this entry, she finds herself investigating the killings of two exotic dancers from Atlanta who were working with Lavotini in a Panama City, Florida, club. Lavotini's romantic interest is in local police detective, John Nailer. Bartholomew blends sex and humor into a alluring mix.

Bruce, Gemma

Who Loves Ya, Baby? 2005. Kensington, ISBN 0758212496, 352p.

Bruce's tale of former NYPD Officer Julie Excelsior, who returns to her upstate roots after she inherits a house from her uncle, deftly mixes an intriguing mystery with some hot romance. Julie reconnects with the boyfriend of her youth, who is now the town sheriff, and their romance rekindles into passion that will leave you breathless. Humor, romance, mystery, and sex, Bruce provides all of these in her fast-paced tale.

Cash, Dixie

My Heart May Be Broken, but My Hair Still Looks Great. **Domestic Equalizer mysteries.** 2006. Avon Trade, ISBN 0061134236, 336p.

Love and mystery mix Texas-style in this series featuring hairdressing detectives Debbie Sue Overstreet and Edwina Perkins-Martin. Whether it's a wayward husband or a horse thief, this lusty pair sets them straight. Here, they are playing matchmaker for a couple of newcomers in town and investigating the disappearance of several valuable horses. The romance gets pretty steamy here from both sides of the gender divide.

Crusie, Jennifer
Fast Women. 2002. St. Martin's Paperbacks, ISBN 0312980159, 436p.

Forty-something Nell Dysart is recently divorced and trying to get her life back on track. When she takes a secretarial job for a detective agency, she finds her love life kicking back into action. The love scenes get pretty graphic as Nell and her office mates engage in private investigations. Nell also finds herself working on an embezzlement case, and then the bodies start turning up. Crusie offers a signature story, filled with sex, witty dialogue, and appealing characters.

Greenwood, Kerry
Urn Burial. **Phryne Fisher mysteries.** 2007. Poisoned Pen Press, ISBN 159058368X, 280p.

In the 1920s, the Victorian mores were beginning to lift, and women were experiencing newfound sexual freedom. That is certainly the case with Greenwood's Phryne Fisher, who is a lusty and intrepid amateur detective in post–World War I Australia. Fisher takes delight in her freedoms and takes time to enjoy her lover in between bouts of sleuthing. Here, Fisher investigates death threats and attacks at an inn where she is vacationing.

Michaels, Kasey
Maggie by the Book. **Maggie Kelly mysteries.** 2004. Kensington, ISBN 1575668823, 352p.

Like her eponymous sleuth, Michaels is a romance writer who has taken up mystery fiction. In Maggie Kelly's case, though, things are complicated when her Regency detective, Alexandre, Viscount St. Just, turns up in her twenty-first-century New York apartment. Michaels builds the romance and mystery in tandem as Maggie is torn between St. Just and her NYPD boyfriend and the bodies pile up at a romance writers convention.

Robb, J. D.
Memory in Death. **Eve Dallas mysteries.** 2006. Berkley, ISBN 0425210731, 384p.

NYPD Lieutenant Eve Dallas and her powerful ex-criminal husband make quite a team in this long-running series set in the mid-twenty-first century. The pair's sexuality has a crucial role in their relationship, and Robb does not hesitate to display it. But it's not all sex and dalliances. Dallas is a tenacious cop, and here she investigates a killing close to home. Her foster mother, who treated Dallas like dirt, shows up looking for money and then is murdered.

Rose, M. J.
➡ *The Delilah Complex*. **Dr. Morgan Snow mysteries.** 2006. Mira, ISBN 0778322157, 384p.

Dr. Snow, a New York sex therapist, is called on to counsel the members of the Scarlet Society, a club of women who like to sexually dominate men.

When a male guest of the club is murdered and a photo of his body sent to the *New York Times,* Snow teams up with NYPD Officer Noah Jordain to uncover the killer. Rose writes highly erotically charged thrillers that explore the dark edges of sexuality.

I'd Like to Buy a Clue:
Chick-Lit Mysteries

The chick-lit phenomenon, which took off after the publication of Helen Fielding's *Bridget Jones's Diary* (1996), has made its way into the crime fiction genre. These stories feature a female protagonist and blend romance (though not always true love), humor, and bright covers (usually pink). Shopping and hip trends are also important pieces of the frame here. This blend creates a mood for the story that captures an urban zeitgeist of the late twentieth and early twenty-first centuries.

Anderson, Sheryl

⇨ *Killer Heels*. **Molly Forrester mysteries.** 2005. St. Martin's Paperbacks, ISBN 0312992564, 320p.

> You know you are in a chick-lit mystery when the first page finds our heroine complaining about the damage to the her shoes from the blood of the corpse that she just found. Molly Forrester is an advice columnist for a hip New York magazine, and then she stumbles across the body of the magazine's advertising director. Between shoe shopping and mojitos, Molly takes on the investigation with a fine sense of humor and a sharp eye for clues.

Bloom, Elizabeth

See Isabelle Run. 2006. Warner Books, ISBN 0446617180, 304p.

> Lots of chick-lit mysteries are set in the publishing world. What better locale for hip fashions, fancy clothes, and murder? By page five of Bloom's fast-moving mystery, we already know that our heroine is wearing an Ann Taylor suit with a pair of Ferragamos, and the name-dropping continues as Isabelle Leonard takes a job with a Martha Stewart-esque multimedia lifestyle firm. But when a series of unexplained deaths strike the company, Isabelle is worried that she might be next and takes on the investigation.

Bond, Stephanie

Body Movers. **Carlotta Wren mysteries.** 2006. Mira, ISBN 0778323331, 432p.

> Carlotta Wren's parents have to go on the lam to avoid prison, leaving her in charge of a younger brother and with no means of support. Sales clerking at Neiman Marcus may not be the best job, but at least it keeps the rent paid and gives her the opportunity to keep up with fashion. Various mysteries are under investigation here, but the pleasure is as much in Bond's humor and witty tone and in the descriptions of the world of expensive clothes.

Cabot, Meg
Size 12 Is Not Fat. **Heather Wells mysteries.** 2005. Avon Trade, ISBN 0060525118, 368p.

> Best known for her Princess Diaries series, chick-lit star Cabot here turns to murder. Heather Wells made it big on the teen music circuit, but now things have taken a bad turn. Her studio has dropped her, as has her boyfriend. In hopes of righting her life, she takes a job at a Manhattan college, but when two students die in suspicious circumstances and the police write it off as an accident, Heather plunges into the hunt for the killer. A fun start to an amusing series.

Davis, Kyra
Sex, Murder, and a Double Latte. **Sophie Katz mysteries.** 2005. Red Dress Ink, ISBN 0373895194, 304p.

> Mystery writer Sophie Katz finds life imitating art when a series of crimes occurs just as she had written them in her novel. What's a girl to do in that case but team up with her buddies and take on the case? Like a good cappuccino, Davis's writing mixes light and dark with a froth of humor and some romantic spice into a delectable blend.

Roberts, Wendy
Dating Can Be Deadly. 2005. Red Dress Ink, ISBN 0373895127, 288p.

> The local bistro is a common setting for chick-lit novels. The heroine and her friends meet there to share hip drinks and kvetch about their lives. Tabitha enjoys the "mysteries of butterscotch schnapps" as much as any girl, but her life is complicated by her psychic powers. She gets caught between a killer and the police when her senses tell her that a murder has been committed nearby. Roberts ably mixes the chick-lit and mystery elements here.

Sturman, Jennifer
The Key. **Rachel Benjamin mysteries.** 2006. Red Dress Ink, ISBN 0373896034, 304p.

> Bosses run a close second to boyfriends as a source of problems in chick-lit novels, but when Rachel Benjamin wishes her boss was dead, she does not really expect to find him poisoned. Now she is the main suspect in the killing and must clear her name. Sturman offers a lively and humorous mix of romance and mystery set in the world of investment banking.

Murder and the Great Beyond: Supernatural Mysteries

Although there are some crime fiction stories that obviously have their roots deeply embedded in the science fiction, fantasy, or horror genres, there is another class of stories that explores the boundary between real and supernatural in a less direct fashion. These stories seek more to raise questions for the reader and to make you wonder about the possibilities that exist beyond the natural world than to scare you. Sometimes funny, sometimes more dark, all the stories here include elements of the supernatural that help propel the story along.

Damsgaard, Shirley

Witch Way to Murder. **Ophelia and Abby mysteries.** 2005. Avon, ISBN 0060793481, 304p.

A librarian detective with psychic abilities, whose grandmother is also a healer and psychic, makes for an appealing character in Damsgaard's cozy series. When a body turns up in the backyard, the pair finds themselves involved in an investigation that expands as the story progresses. Readers looking for a mix of romance, mystery, and humor with a tinge of the supernatural will find a lot to enjoy here.

DePoy, Phillip

The Devil's Hearth. **Fever Devilin mysteries.** 2004. Worldwide Library, ISBN 0373264925, 272p.

The Appalachians are filled with stories of haunts and odd happenings. Folklorist Fever Devilin has returned to his home in the Georgia mountains, only to find a dead body on the porch of his family cabin. As he looks into the killing with a childhood friend, now a deputy sheriff, Devilin finds the spirits of the past mingling with the deeds of the present in this eerie and fascinating story.

Grabien, Deborah

Matty Groves. **English Ballad mysteries.** 2005. St. Martin's Minotaur, ISBN 0312333897, 256p.

Like author Sharyn McCrumb, Grabien uses folk songs as the foundation for her eerie mystery series featuring singer Ringan Laine. When Laine and his ensemble are asked to play at a manor house in Hampshire, England, they find themselves in the middle of an unsolved mystery that has left the house haunted by spirits. A fine addition to Grabien's series.

Gruber, Michael

Night of the Jaguar. **Jimmy Paz mysteries.** 2007. Harper, ISBN 006057769X, 432p.

Strange dreams have been troubling the sleep of retired cop Jimmy Paz, ones that revolve around killing and revenge. And the dreams seem to come to life when Paz is brought back to investigate a series of killings that appear to have a supernatural origin. Like the magical realists of Latin America, Gruber erases the boundaries between the real and the uncanny in this thrilling mystery.

McCrumb, Sharyn

⇨ *She Walks These Hills*. **Ballad mysteries.** 1995. Signet, ISBN 0451184726, 448p.

McCrumb's mysteries all turn on the intersections of the old and the new, and time seems somewhat permeable in the Appalachian mountain settings for the stories. Here, a 200-year-old story of a woman's escape from Indian captivity provides the foundation for the contemporary mysteries investigated by Sheriff Arrowood and his force. Like a great ballad singer, McCrumb skillfully merges melody, plot, and character into a coherent whole.

Shuman, George
18 Seconds. 2007. Pocket Star, ISBN 0743277171, 384p.

Sherry Moore was blinded in an accident, which also left her with an odd ability. She puts her hand on a corpse and sees what they saw in the last moments of life. It's a disturbing gift, but it occasionally proves useful to criminal investigations. When a serial killer begins preying on young girls in a New Jersey town, the lead investigator calls on Moore for assistance. Shuman offers a creepy police procedural with a touch of the paranormal.

Skibbins, David
Eight of Swords. **Tarot card mysteries.** 2006. St. Martin's Minotaur, ISBN 0312352255, 288p.

Sixties radical Warren Ritter is still hiding out for his activities 30 years after the revolution did not materialize. He now offers tarot readings in Berkeley to support himself. When a young woman gets a daunting reading and then disappears, Ritter must figure out what has happened without jeopardizing his own freedom. A strong sense of place, interesting characters, and a dash of New Age mysticism make this series a good pick.

Dark Night of the Soul:
The Noir Mystery

There has always been an undercurrent of desolation and despair that runs through the crime fiction genre. Noir thrillers have been popular since the days of the pulp magazine, but as the twentieth century faded into the twenty-first, mean streets and damaged detectives experienced a resurgence. In many ways, these stories reflect the growing concerns of contemporary society about safety, community, and values. The titles listed here all share a bleak outlook on the human condition.

Burke, James Lee
A Morning for Flamingos. **Dave Robicheaux mysteries.** 1991. Avon, ISBN 0380713608, 384p.

Burke's novels consistently explore the darker edges of life. Dave Robicheaux, a former New Orleans cop, who has rejoined the force, faces a variety of demons, including the death of his wife, alcohol, and a propensity for violence. The mood of all of Burke's books is somber, but *A Morning for Flamingos* is particularly so, as Robicheaux goes back to the Big Easy and must confront his past.

Kaminsky, Stuart

Retribution. **Lew Fonesca mysteries.** 2002. Forge, ISBN 0812540360, 256p.

Kaminsky's Lew Fonesca leads a dark existence. The death of his wife has left Fonesca in the depths of depression, and he has left his native Chicago for Florida, where he works as a process server. In this entry, Fonesca is looking for two missing persons, a teenage girl and an elderly woman. Both investigations put Fonesca in danger, and this melancholy man makes his way as best he can toward justice.

Khadra, Yasmina

Autumn of the Phantoms. **Inspector Llob mysteries.** 2006. Toby Press, ISBN 1592641431, 132p.

A strong sense of melancholy pervades the third entry in Khadra's mystery series set in Algeria. There is less mystery story here than in the earlier titles and more of a depiction of the hopelessness that political corruption and years of violence have wrought on an Algiers police official, Inspector Llob, and on the country. An essentially good man, Llob cannot seem to find hope of redemption in this dark story.

Lehane, Dennis

⇨ *A Drink before the War*. **Patrick Kenzie and Angela Gennaro mysteries.** 1996. HarperTorch, ISBN 0380726238, 400p.

Lehane writes fast-paced, dark-edged mystery stories set in Boston. The novels are replete with racial tension, the pressures of poverty, and violence that does not distinguish between good people and bad people. The relentless brutality of life in working-class Boston is at the heart of this story in which two Boston PIs confront political corruption and warring gangs.

MacBride, Stuart

Cold Granite. **Logan Lazarus McRae mysteries.** 2006. St. Martin's Minotaur, ISBN 0312940599, 480p.

Set in the gray streets of Aberdeen, Scotland, in the cold winter rains, MacBride's debut mystery could hardly be drearier. The setting and the weather are echoed in the bleak story, which finds Detective Sergeant McRae investigating a series of child killings. The dark mood created by the setting and the story is somewhat offset by the apparent normality of McRae, but be aware that this is a grim tale.

Mankell, Henning

Faceless Killers. **Kurt Wallander mysteries.** 2003. Vintage, ISBN 1400031575, 288p.

In Mankell's second Kurt Wallander mystery, the harshness of a Swedish winter is matched by the somberness of Wallander's personal life. Both of these aspects create a dark and dour feeling for the story. Wallander's wife has left him, he is drinking too much, and his elderly father is declining. His life is complicated when he is called on to investigate the brutal killing of an elderly farming couple, apparently by recent immigrants. A strong sense of Nordic dreariness pervades the book.

Perry, Anne
The Face of a Stranger. **William Monk mysteries.** 1995. Ivy Books, ISBN 9995495600, 345p.

Perry is known for her two series of Victorian mysteries. This is the more somber of the pair, with its unremitting exposure of the grim side of life in nineteenth-century London. Perry describes in detail the hopeless lives of many of London's residents. The mood is exacerbated by her detective's loss of memory. A head injury has left William Monk without a memory, and the novel portrays parallel investigations as Monk uncovers the reason a young aristocrat was murdered and uncovers his own past.

Pronzini, Bill
Mourners. **Nameless Detective mysteries.** 2007. Forge, ISBN 0765349264, 288p.

Pronzini's Nameless Detective has been a favorite of noir readers since the early 1980s. Nameless is the quintessential PI, a good man, who, though plagued by difficulties, is committed to seeking justice in an unjust world. Set in San Francisco, the series is pervaded by a sense of lost innocence and sadness, especially in *Mourners,* in which everyone seems to be grieving a loss.

Rankin, Ian
Knots and Crosses. **Inspector Rebus mysteries.** 1995. St. Martin's Paperbacks, ISBN 0312956738, 228p.

Scottish Police Inspector John Rebus is a dark man. He is divorced, alienated from his family, smokes and drinks to excess, and has few friends on the Edinburgh police force. It is the search for justice for the victims of horrific crimes that redeems him. Rebus's own dark mood is amply matched by Rankin's harsh depictions of the lives of the poor and working class in dim and dreary Edinburgh.

Laughing in the Face of Death: Felonious Humor

After you have read enough crime fiction featuring damaged detectives living lives soaked in alcohol and contemplating the dark side of human nature, you might be ready for a few laughs. Although murder in the real world is never a joking matter, the authors on this list all focus their efforts as much on creating a light mood as on fashioning an interesting mystery story. That does mean that the mystery is secondary, but these detectives all have a sense of humor and put that humor to good use in their investigations.

Andrews, Donna

No Nest for the Wicket. **Meg Langslow mysteries.** 2006. St. Martin's Minotaur, ISBN 0312329407, 272p.

The titles of Andrews's books give you a hint that these are pretty light-hearted mysteries. Bad puns are always a good sign. Andrews builds her humor around a funny and eccentric cast of characters, beginning with black-smith and amateur sleuth Meg Langslow and her family. Here, Meg takes up extreme croquet, but when she finds a body in the rough, it presents a sticky wicket for her.

Cannell, Dorothy

The Importance of Being Ernestine. **Ellie Haskell mysteries.** 2003. Penguin, ISBN 0142002844, 256p.

The laughs are more subtle perhaps in Cannell's humorous British take on the PI novel. Cannell's series heroine Ellie Haskell is visiting her housekeeper, who also cleans the office of a local PI, when a potential client walks in, and Ellie and Mrs. Malloy decide that they can handle the case on their own. The characters and dialogue add to the humor.

Crider, Bill

Mammoth Murder. **Sheriff Dan Rhodes mysteries.** 2006. St. Martin's Minotaur, ISBN 0312323875, 272p.

A folksy policeman and small-town atmosphere are the trademarks of Crider's Sheriff Rhodes mysteries set in rural Texas. Rhodes has a great ear for humorous dialogue, and his Blacklin County, Texas, residents are an amiable bunch of eccentrics, including Bud Turley, who brings in a tooth to the sheriff and claims that it is from Bigfoot and that he found it out in the woods near town. When a friend of Turley's turns up dead shortly thereafter and other murders ensue, Rhodes has a lot on his hands.

Evanovich, Janet

⇨ *Four to Score*. **Stephanie Plum mysteries.** 1998. St. Martin's Paperbacks, ISBN 0312966970, 338p.

If you are looking for mysteries with laugh-out-loud moments, then the adventures of bail bondswoman Stephanie Plum should meet your needs. Sassy dialogue, improbable situations, and wild characters make a high-octane humor blend. *Four to Score* finds Stephanie tracking down "skips" with the aid of a 6'8" transvestite and a retired hooker who packs a variety of heat. The jokes come at a nonstop pace.

Hess, Joan

Muletrain to Maggody. **Arly Hanks mysteries.** 2004. Pocket, ISBN 0743443896, 336p.

Like Garrison Keillor, Hess mines the lives of the residents of her small town of Maggody, Arkansas, for gentle humor. Unlike Lake Wobegon, though,

Maggody seems to have a high proportion of violent deaths in addition to the humor. Here, lost Confederate gold, a bunch of Civil War reenactors, and some mysterious deaths make for a delightfully cozy mystery for Sheriff Arly Hanks and her fellow townsfolk.

Levine, Laura
This Pen for Hire. **Jaine Austen mysteries.** 2003. Kensington, ISBN 0758201591, 240p.

LA's hipster scene offers Levine an ample palette for satire, and she makes the most of it in her Jaine Austen mysteries. Jaine (her mother loved English literature but was a bad speller) is a Los Angeles writer who is free-lancing until her break comes. When she pens a love letter for a client and the object of his affection turns up dead, Jaine feels obliged to prove him innocent. Levine has a sharp eye for pretension and leaves few LA sacred cows untouched by her wit.

Yancey, Richard
The Highly Effective Detective. 2006. St. Martin's Minotaur, ISBN 0312347529, 304p.

He's 33, he flunked out of police training, and works as a security guard. So when Theodore Ruzak's mother dies and leaves him a bundle of cash, he does what he always wanted to do and opens a detective agency. Unfortunately, his ambition is not matched by his skills. Teddy raises investigative incompetence to new heights, but he is a sweet guy whose charm grows on you. Yancey creates a fun blend of humor and thrills.

The Robot Did It, or Perhaps It Was the Unicorn: Mysteries for Speculative Fiction Fans

Although crime fiction has long since cross-pollinated with romance and historical fiction, it has been slower to branch out into fantasy and science fiction. But in the last few years, a number of writers have taken crime fiction down the Yellow Brick Road, into the world of artificial intelligence, or off to the stars. Here are some of the best of these genre-blending efforts.

Andrews, Donna
You've Got Murder. **Turing Hopper mysteries.** 2003. Berkley, ISBN 0425189457, 304p.

Andrews moves beyond the flesh-and-blood detective in introducing readers to Turing Hopper, an Artificial Intelligence Personality. Set in an indeterminate, but not too distant, future, Turing is located at the Universal Library and has a seemingly endless set of connections to other networks and to

Universal's omnipresent security cameras. Turing recruits two human side-kicks, Watsons to her Holmes, and together they investigate the disappearance of her programmer.

Fforde, Jasper
The Big Over Easy. **Nursery Crimes mysteries.** 2006. Penguin, ISBN 0143037234, 400p.

In a world where Bo Peep and the Gingerbread Man mingle with the rest of the citizens of Reading, England, Detective Jack Spratt and Officer Mary Mary are responsible for keeping order among the nursery characters. The murder of Humpty Dumpty provides the meat of the plot, and Fforde scrambles fantasy, puns, and mystery into a delightful dish.

Garcia, Eric
Anonymous Rex. **Vincent Rubio mysteries.** 2003. Berkley, ISBN 0425188884, 368p.

In a brilliant twist on the hard-boiled PI novel, Garcia creates a world where dinosaurs did not die out and just evolved the ability to disguise them-selves and coexist among the human population. A down-at-the-heel veloci-raptor, Vince Rubio, is working as a PI and stumbles across evidence of bizarre experiments to crossbreed the dinosaur and human populations. *Anonymous Rex* provides an interesting variant on LA noir.

Gibson, William, and Bruce Sterling
The Difference Engine. 1992. Spectra, ISBN 055329461X, 448p.

In an alternative England during the reign of Victoria, Babbage's engine is a working reality, and Lord Byron is prime minister. Science and rationalism rule the day, but their reign is challenged by Luddite conspiracies. A set of punch cards that could destabilize society is at the heart of the mystery, and conspiracies abound in this clever blending of alternative history, science fiction, and crime.

Grimwood, Jon
⇨ *Pashazade*. **Arabesk mysteries.** 2005. Spectra, ISBN 0553587439, 384p.

Parallel stories set in the twenty-first century outline the life of ZeeZee, who also is known as Ashraf al-Mansur. As Ashraf, he finds himself accused, of murder in the major city of the still extant Ottoman Empire, and he goes underground to clear himself. Grimwood presents an intriguing blend of alter-native history and mystery, with a most appealing main character.

Harrison, Kim
Dead Witch Walking. **Rachel Morgan mysteries.** 2004. Eos, ISBN 0060572965, 432p.

Harrison's series features witch and investigator Rachel Morgan. In a Cin-cinnati where the humans live side by side with supernatural beings, Morgan tracks down paranormal crime. She's on the outs with her boss, though, and can't get any good assignments. So Morgan pairs up with a vampire and a pixie to bring down a corrupt politician to prove her skills. Paranormal mystery blends with humor in this first of a series.

Pratchett, Terry
Men at Arms. **Discworld novels.** 1997. HarperTorch, ISBN 0061092193, 400p.

Pratchett's Discworld stories are set in a world that vaguely resembles preindustrial England. Several of the books follow the travails of the City Watch under the leadership of Captain Sam Vimes. Pratchett has a great affection for the police procedural, and his team of officers is as believable as any big-city precinct, though you don't usually find dwarves, trolls, werewolves, and zombies in the NYPD.

Scare You to Death: Crime and Punishment for Horror Fans

Although crime fiction often offers thrills and excitement, there are a number of authors who are upping readers' pulse rates by including elements of horror in their mysteries. The stories in this list all feature elements of the occult or supernatural that can make the hair stand up on your neck as well as tell a gripping crime story. You might want to read these in the daylight.

Butcher, Jim
Dead Beat. **Dresden mysteries.** 2006. Roc, ISBN 045146091X, 448p.

Harry Dresden is a Chicago PI with a difference: He is also a wizard and dedicated to protecting Chicago from the denizens of the dark. He works with Detective Karrin Murphy of the Chicago PD's Special Investigations Division (they take care of the supernatural side of policing). Dresden and Murphy are faced with vampires, necromancers, and a lost occult text that could lead to world domination for whoever finds it. It's a chilling tale leavened by a dash of dark humor.

Connolly, John
⇨ *Dark Hollow*. **Charlie "Bird" Parker mysteries.** 2002. Pocket, ISBN 074341022X, 528p.

The comparisons to Stephen King seem to be particularly appropriate for this dark tale of detection and the supernatural. Like King, Connolly creates an eerily believable situation in which the uncanny seems all too real. Serial killings old and new haunt PI Charlie Parker, who has returned to his Maine hometown after the deaths of his wife and son. The evil is palpable in this chilling tale.

Elrod, P. N.
Cold Streets. **Vampire Files mysteries.** 2003. Ace, ISBN 0441011039, 384p.

Chicago in the 1930s, with its gangsters, nightclubs, and PIs, might be enough for most writers, but Elrod ups the ante by making her lead a vampire as well, and a reluctant one at that. A mix of horror and humor propels the story as Jack Fleming, our vampire hero, part-time detective, and owner of a nightclub, breaks up a kidnapping, faces a blackmailer, and resists a Mob takeover of Jack's club.

Harris, Charlaine

Grave Sight. **Harper Connelly mysteries.** 2006. Berkley, ISBN 0425212890, 320p.

Harper Connelly was struck by lightening, which left her with the ability to sense death and to re-create the last moments of the dead person. She ekes out a precarious living tracking down missing persons, traveling with her stepbrother from town to town. When they are called to the town of Sarne, Arkansas, to help locate a missing teen, Harper finds her body, but the town has secrets that the inhabitants would prefer stay buried.

James, Peter

Dead Simple. 2007. Carroll and Graf, ISBN 0786718498, 416p.

In this highly disturbing blend of horror and crime fiction, a stag night prank goes bad, leaving a bridegroom buried alive. The story alternates between the bridegroom, the police who are looking for him, and his amoral business partner, who has some dark secrets. A strong sense of evil pervades the entire story, and there are some chilling characters that are hard to forget, as much as you might like to do so.

Miyabe, Miyuki

Crossfire. 2006. Oxford University Press, ISBN 4770029934, 408p.

Paranormal powers are the focus of Miyabe's mix of occult and police procedural. Junko Aoki has the ability to light up the world, literally, as she can set anything ablaze with a thought. But power can corrupt, and Junko becomes a vigilante, burning those she suspects of crimes. Police Officer Chikako Ishizu is investigating the series of suspicious fires and killings, and Miyabe tells a suspense-filled tale with some horrific moments.

Waggoner, Tim

Necropolis. 2004. Five Star Trade, ISBN 1410402150, 248p.

Finding this world too much to handle, the denizens of the dark founded their own city, Necropolis. A former earthly police officer, Matthew Adrion, is now a zombie PI in the city of the dead. In a bewitching mix of horror and hard-boiled detective story, Waggoner includes more dark humor than the other writers in this list, but the paranormal plotline and a cast of the undead will keep horror fans reading.

Chapter Five

Language

Language is one of the hardest appeal factors to gauge, both for readers and for readers' advisors. This is, in part, because the appreciation of language is so subjective. One reader's lyrical, descriptive novel is another's boring, long-winded story. What seems elegant style to one reader may strike a different reader as purple prose. Language appeals can include things like the length of the book, the speed with which the reader gets through the story, special items that the writer chooses to include in the book, and how the author uses dialogue and humor. Although critics are getting better about mentioning theses sorts of things in reviews, it still can be difficult to come up with read-alikes based on language. The following lists are a place to start for both readers and readers' advisors.

The Canting Crew: The Sounds of the Street

Some writers excel at capturing the slang of the streets and using the criminal argot to create the atmosphere of the story. Whether they are contemporary crime novels with rough language and rougher characters or historical mysteries that use the "flash" language of the criminal class to take you back in time, the stories on this list all have a certain linguistic turn of phrase.

Alexander, Bruce
Person or Persons Unknown. **Sir John Fielding mysteries.** 1998. Berkley, ISBN 0425165663, 336p.

Alexander deftly captures the sounds and sights of eighteenth-century London in his Sir John Fielding series. Alexander's ear for language adds to the atmosphere of the story, and he understands the way speech defined class in the period. Here, in particular, Alexander makes use of those distinctions as Fielding and his assistant, Jeremy Proctor, investigate the murders of prostitutes in London's Covent Garden.

Crichton, Michael
⇨ *The Great Train Robbery.* 2002. Avon, ISBN 0060502304, 352p.

Better known for his science-based thrillers, Crichton can also spin a fine historical mystery. Here, he tells of a plot to steal a military payroll as it is transported across England via train. The story is based on the 1855 robbery of the South Eastern Railway, and Crichton sets the stage with his immense vocabulary of nineteenth-century criminal argot. If you want to know what a prigger of prauncers does, Crichton is your man.

Gash, Jonathan
Prey Dancing. **Clare Burtonall mysteries.** 1999. Penguin, ISBN 0140280162, 288p.

Gash moves from his lighthearted Lovejoy novels to a much darker scene, and his use of criminal vernacular sets a somber tone to this story. Here, the denseness of the slang adds to the lowering atmosphere of the story. A promise to a dying AIDS patient leads English physician Dr. Clare Burtonall into a seamy and dangerous underworld of drugs, prostitution, and murder.

Mosley, Walter
A Little Yellow Dog. **Easy Rawlins mysteries.** 1997. Pocket, ISBN 0671884298, 336p.

Mosley's Easy Rawlins stories are mostly set in Los Angeles between the 1940s and the 1960s. Rawlins is a somewhat reluctant private eye, who takes on investigations as much out of a sense of responsibility as for the money. As Rawlins moves between the African American and white communities of LA, Mosley uses language to define characters and captures the sounds of Southern California's seedy side.

Vachss, Andrew
Footsteps of the Hawk. **Burke mysteries.** 1996. Vintage, ISBN 0679766634, 256p.

Vachss's dark and brooding Burke mysteries are replete with the sounds of the street. The stories here are violent and edged with cruelty, and the language of the characters echoes that violence. Vachss's ear for the rough language of the urban criminal rings true. Here, Burke battles both corrupt cops and a vicious serial killer in his usual avenger style.

Westlake, Donald
> *What's the Worst that Could Happen?* **Dortmunder mysteries.** 2001. Mysterious Press, ISBN 089296586X, 304p.
>
>> Comic caper mysteries usually abound with criminal dialogue, and Westlake is a master of the lingo of small-time crooks. Dortmunder is Westlake's hapless but energetic thief, and here he assembles a team to exact revenge on a wealthy businessman who caught Dortmunder in midburglary and stole Dortmunder's lucky ring.

Conversation Killers:
High-Dialogue Crime Fiction

Some crime fiction writers really have a gift for creating dialogue. Conversations between the characters drive the story, enhancing the believability of the characters and helping set the stage for the investigation. Sometimes witty, sometimes serious, the authors on this list all have an ear for natural dialogue that shapes their stories.

Beechey, Alan
> *An Embarrassment of Corpses.* **Oliver Swithin mysteries.** 1997. Thomas Dunne Books, ISBN 0312169361, 265p.
>
>> Readers looking for English wit and wordplay will enjoy the crisp dialogue and witty language of Beechey's Oliver Swithin mysteries. Here, Swithin comes across a corpse in Trafalgar Square. At first taken as an accident, the death is only the first in a series of killings in London, and children's book writer Swithin steps in to investigate.

Calder, James
> *Knockout Mouse.* **Bill Damen mysteries.** 2002. Chronicle Books, ISBN 0811834999, 272p.
>
>> Filmmaker Bill Damen lives in Silicon Valley and shoots documentaries and promotional films. The death of a guest at a dinner he is attending prompts Damen to investigate, leading him into the shadowy world of biotech and genetic engineering. Calder has an ear for the rhythms of speech in the high-tech world of entrepreneurs and their hangers-on.

Coben, Harlan
> *Drop Shot.* **Myron Bolitar mysteries.** 2002. Orion Paperbacks, ISBN 075284914X, 384p.
>
>> Coben understands the world of sports, and his Myron Bolitar mysteries ring with the sounds of athletes, agents, and wannabes talking to and at one another. Coben's stories move briskly, propelled by the language. Here, Bolitar investigates the shooting of a female tennis star, and the dialogue moves as quickly as a rally at the net.

Davis, Lindsey

The Silver Pigs. **Marcus Didius Falco mysteries.** 2006. St. Martin's Minotaur, ISBN 031235777X, 352p.

Imagine one of the classic hard-boiled detectives dropped into imperial Rome, and you will have grasped the essence of Davis's Falco mysteries. These fast-paced stories run on dialogue and feature smart-mouthed investigator Marcus Didius Falco and a host of other cleverly depicted characters. A chance encounter with a girl in the Forum puts Falco on the trail of stolen imperial silver in this early entry in the series.

Greenwood, Kerry

The Castlemaine Murders. **Phryne Fisher mysteries.** 2006. Poisoned Pen Press, ISBN 1590582802, 252p.

An unusual milieu (1920s Australia) and a free-spirited main character are a good start for a fine historical mystery story. Add in a bit of sex and some witty repartee and you have the recipe for Greenwood's Phryne Fisher mysteries. In this entry in the series, a trip to an amusement park turns up a real body hidden inside a midway attraction.

Hammett, Dashiell

⇨ *The Thin Man.* 1989. Vintage, ISBN 0679722637, 208p.

Elegant as a tuxedo and filled with witty banter, Hammett's *The Thin Man* was quite a shift from his early hard-boiled mysteries. Here, Nick and Nora Charles enjoy the life of the wealthy, frequenting hotel suites and speakeasies, and the alcohol flows as freely as the wit. A chance meeting with the daughter of a former client leads the pair into a murder investigation.

Lawrence, David

The Dead Sit Around in a Ring. **Stella Mooney mysteries.** 2003. Penguin, ISBN 0141004878, 448p.

A gritty, dark police procedural featuring English police officer Stella Mooney. Detective Mooney's investigations take her into the rough side of London, far from the tourist attractions. Lawrence has an ear for speech that adds to the bleak feeling of the story, as Mooney investigates the murder of a small-time con man that has been disguised as a suicide.

Lingering On and On: High-Page-Count Mysteries

Sometimes you want a mystery story that takes a more leisurely route to the solution of the crime. Often it is the lyrical, descriptive language that slows the book down, drawing you in and setting a lush foundation for the story. The titles on this list all offer you the opportunity to luxuriate in the story and enjoy an extended visit with the characters.

Chabon, Michael
The Yiddish Policeman's Union. 2007. HarperCollins, ISBN 0007149824, 414p.

Sitka, Alaska, home of refugees from the Holocaust and the collapse of Israel in 1948, is the setting for Chabon's mystery that is part hard-boiled detective story, part romance, and part meditation on the nature of Jewish culture and life. Chabon's elegiac style matches the tone of the story, as the residents of the federal district of Sitka prepare for reintegration back into the United States. Sitka detective Meyer Landsman investigates the murder of a neighbor in this moving and thoughtful mystery.

Eco, Umberto
The Name of the Rose. 2006. Everyman's Library, ISBN 0307264890, 600p.

With its blending of history, detection, religion, and occult knowledge, Eco's mystery offers myriad interests for readers looking to immerse themselves in a mystery story. Set in the 1320s, the story centers on an investigation into heresy charges in an Italian monastery. A twisting plot, fascinating characters, and lyrical writing demand the reader's attention, but it is well worth the effort.

James, P. D.
The Murder Room. **Adam Dalgliesh mysteries.** 2004. Vintage, ISBN 1400076099, 432p.

James's lyrical writing and her understanding of English police procedure add to both the enjoyment and the heft of her Dalgliesh mysteries. The care that James gives to the development of her characters also necessitates a longer story. Here, Dalgliesh and his team from Scotland Yard investigate murders surrounding the fate of a small museum.

Janes, J. Robert
Mayhem. **Jean-Louis St. Cyr and Hermann Kohler mysteries.** 1999. Soho Crime, ISBN 1569471584, 272p.

Sometimes even a relatively short book (by page count) can be a slow read. Here, Janes's descriptive language and brooding tone bring a more deliberate pace to what could have been a breakneck thriller. Set in Occupied France, the series features Sûreté Detective St. Cyr, who is paired with Gestapo officer Kohler. The pair investigates a killing that their bosses want written off as a Resistance killing, and Kohler and St. Cyr's refusal to whitewash the murder puts them in danger.

Liss, David
A Conspiracy of Paper. **Benjamin Weaver mysteries.** 2001. Ballantine, ISBN 0804119120, 480p.

Historical mysteries often take a more leisurely approach to detection. The authors are eager to set the stage with detailed descriptions of the setting and time period. Liss's book fits that pattern, with eighteenth-century London coming to life in all its filth and splendor. Prizefighter and thief taker Benjamin

Weaver here investigates the murder of his father. Liss has an ear for the language and history but never succumbs to pedantry.

Nesser, Hakan
    Borkmann's Point. **Inspector Van Veeteren mysteries.** 2007. Vintage, ISBN 1400030323, 336p.

        Not all hard-boiled mysteries race from scene to scene propelled by violence and alcohol. The increasingly popular Scandinavian school of crime fiction mixes tough but reflective investigators, lyrical depictions of nature, and a slower pace. Nesser's first novel introduces Chief Inspector Van Veeteren of the Stockholm police, whose vacation is interrupted when he is asked to investigate a series of murders in an isolated community.

Pears, Iain
    ⇨ *An Instance of the Fingerpost*. 1999. Berkley, ISBN 0425167720, 752p.

        The complex plot and vast array of characters may leave some readers bewildered, but Pears's historical mystery, set in seventeenth-century England, is a tour de force that blends espionage, science, religion, and detection. The book looks at the murder of Oxford professor Robert Grove through the eyes of four different narrators. In the end, it is hard to say which of them has the truth of the matter.

Sansom, C. J.
    Dark Fire. **Matthew Shardlake mysteries.** 2005. Penguin, ISBN 0143036432, 512p.

        Sansom offers up an absorbing blend of political intrigue, theological controversy, courtroom drama, complex plotting, and mystery in this lengthy historical thriller featuring sixteenth-century lawyer Matthew Shardlake and his assistant Jack Barak. The pair is charged by Thomas Cromwell, Henry VIII's chief minister, to discover the secret of Greek fire, a weapon of unparalleled terror that Cromwell hopes will get him back in Henry's graces. A parallel plot presents Shardlake defending a young girl on a murder charge for killing her cousin.

A Speedy Death: Fast-Paced Crimes and Criminals

At the other end of the spectrum are those crime novels that speed by like a getaway car fleeing the scene of a bank heist. It might be the cinematic cutting of the story, the breakneck pace of the plot, or lots of fast-moving dialogue, but in all cases the titles listed here take crime fiction fans on a fast-paced jaunt through detection. Whether you are looking for a book to finish on a plane flight or one that you can enjoy on a lazy afternoon, you'll find some good possibilities here.

Anderson, Sheryl

Killer Deal. **Molly Forrester mysteries.** 2006. St. Martin's Minotaur, ISBN 0312350058, 320p.

Propelled by dialogue and featuring tight plotting, Anderson's Molly Forrester stories are definitely quick reads. Forrester is a writer for a New York lifestyle magazine who wants to be a crime writer. Here, she investigates the murder of an ad executive, supported by two friends. Her boyfriend, NYPD Detective Kyle Edwards, wants Molly to drop the investigation to keep herself safe, but she perseveres.

Connors, Rose

False Testimony. **Marty Nickerson mysteries.** 2006. Pocket Star, ISBN 0743492706, 352p.

Courtroom mysteries tend to move quickly, with the action shifting from defense to prosecution in a cinematic style. This is certainly the case in Connors's fast-paced story that finds defense attorney Marty Nickerson involved in two cases: defending a U.S. senator whose young aide has gone missing and sitting as a court-appointed attorney for a young man accused of killing a priest. The short chapters and carefully crafted dialogue move the story along briskly.

Levine, Laura

The PMS Murder. **Jaine Austen mysteries.** 2007. Kensington, ISBN 0758207840, 256p.

An informal, first-person narration and witty dialogue moves Levine's mysteries at a brisk pace. When LA freelance writer Jaine Austen is invited to join a women's support group (drinking and comparing lost loves), she accepts the invitation, but one of the group is murdered, and Jaine and the other members are under suspicion. Jaine steps in to clear herself and unmask the real criminal in this charming, funny tale.

Muller, Marcia

⇨ *Vanishing Point.* **Sharon McCone mysteries.** 2006. Mysterious Press, ISBN 0892968052, 336p.

Not all quick-read mysteries are frothy cozies. Muller's stories star tough PI Sharon McCone and often deal with difficult issues. But the rapid pace of the dialogue and the careful plotting move the stories along. Here, McCone investigates a cold-case disappearance that is complicated when her client also disappears. Interesting plots and strong characters make this a strong series.

Preston, Douglas, and Lincoln Child

The Dance of Death. **Pendergast trilogy.** 2006. Warner Books, ISBN 0446617091, 592p.

Preston and Child's books are proof that the speed of the read is not necessarily related to the number of pages. Even at almost 600 pages, this entry in the battle between FBI agent Aloysius Pendergast and his demonic brother

Diogenes races by. The cinematic structure of the story moves you quickly from scene to scene, and the thrills are nonstop. You'll be finished and on to book three before you know it.

Robb, J. D.

Survivor in Death. **Eve Dallas mysteries.** 2005. Berkley, ISBN 0425204189, 384p.

In this series (by Nora Roberts writing as J. D. Robb), the suspense and action keep you turning the pages. Set in the second half of the twenty-first century, the stories have some futuristic elements, but it is Robb's blend of interesting characters, romantic tension, and a tightly plotted mystery that make this a fun series. Here, Dallas investigates the mass murder of a family while she cares for a young girl, the only surviving member of the family.

Sedley, Kate

The Three Kings of Cologne. **Roger the Chapman mysteries.** 2007. Severn House, ISBN 0727864815, 252p.

Not all historical mysteries are leisurely strolls through the past. Sedley's series follows itinerant peddler Roger the Chapman on his peregrinations across fifteenth-century England. Dialogue driven and filled with interesting characters, the stories include enough detail to make them believable, but not so much as to slow down the pace of the investigation. Here, Roger is asked to investigate the discovery of the body of a woman who disappeared two decades earlier.

Todd, Marilyn

Sour Grapes. **Claudia Seferius mysteries.** 2006. Severn House, ISBN 0727863177, 249p.

Todd is another historical crime fiction writer whose series, featuring Roman widow Claudia Seferius, moves along smartly, due in large part to the witty banter between the characters. Lighter on the historical detail than some Roman period crime fiction (think Steven Saylor), Todd nonetheless conjures up a brisk tale of murder and revenge in imperial Tuscany.

Time for Just One: Great Mystery Story Collections

There are occasions when you do not have the time to read an entire novel, even a fast-paced one. Fortunately for crime fiction aficionados, the field is replete with fine mystery short stories from the pens of many of the best-known crime novelists. These shorter efforts still contain the excitement of the investigation and the unraveling of a mystery, but it is in a package that you can read in those precious moments of spare time. From cozy to hard-boiled, crime fiction readers will find something to enjoy in these anthologies.

Confederacy of Crime. Sarah Shankman, ed. 2001. Signet, ISBN 0451202198, 304p.

Here's a set of stories for readers who enjoy the quirky characters, red-clay settings, and social issues of Southern crime fiction. With tales from such noted mystery writers as Margaret Maron, Joan Hess, Michael Malone, Jeffery Deaver, and Sarah Shankman, this is a great introduction to regional crime writing at its best.

⇨ *First Cases: First Appearances of Classic Private Eyes.* Robert J. Randisi, ed. 1997. Signet, ISBN 0451190165, 272p.

The First Cases series anthologizes the short story debuts of a variety of crime investigators. This first entry in the series offers up the introductory cases of such well-known PIs as Kinsey Millhone, Matthew Scudder, Amos Walker, and V. I. Warshawski. Other series titles cover amateur detectives, famous detectives, and classic cases. A great start for those readers interested in a variety of crime writing.

Malice Domestic 10. Nevada Barr, ed. 2001. Avon Books, ISBN 0380804840, 212p.

The Malice Domestic series brings together some of the best writers of contemporary cozy mysteries. The 10th entry in the series features stories from Simon Brett, Carolyn Hart, Peter Lovesey, Anne Perry, Nancy Pickard, Margaret Maron, and others. A great source for cozy fans.

Murder among Friends. The Adams Round Table. 2003. Berkley, ISBN 0425192652, 288p.

The Adams Round Table, founded by Mary Higgins Clark, is a collection of crime fiction writers who gather monthly to discuss their profession. This collection offers some fine mystery writing from members of the roundtable. You will find new stories here from Lawrence Block, Mary Higgins Clark, Susan Isaacs, Peter Straub, and others.

Murder in Baker Street. Martin Harry Greenberg et al., eds. 2001. Carroll and Graf, ISBN 0786708980, 277p.

Sherlock Holmes continues to solve mysteries long after the death of his creator, Arthur Conan Doyle. In this entry to the burgeoning selection of Holmesiana, well-known mystery writers Anne Perry, Loren Estleman, Stuart Kaminsky, Peter Tremayne, and others bring Holmes and Watson back to life. There are numerous other Holmes collections that might be of interest, including the Christmas-focused titles in *Holmes for the Holidays*, edited by Martin Harry Greenberg (1998, Berkley, ISBN 0425167542).

Passport to Crime: The Finest Mystery Stories from International Crime Writers. Janet Hutchings, ed. 2006. Carroll and Graf, ISBN 0786719168, 432p.

A great way to locate new and interesting writers is to look at anthologies. If you are intrigued by the recent run of crime fiction by international writers but don't know where to start, this collection offers some jumping-off points. It features stories from top writers from Europe, Latin America, Africa, and Japan. Whether you like police procedurals or humorous historicals, this collection will have something for you.

Shakespearean Detectives. Mike Ashley, ed. 1998. Carroll and Graf, ISBN 0786705965, 412p.

If you enjoy Shakespeare or historical mysteries (or both), you should give *Shakespearean Detectives* a try. Noted mystery writers, including Edward Marston, Susanna Gregory, Margaret Frazer, Peter Tremayne, and others, offer their takes on the stories behind the plays and the characters. The stories are firmly rooted in the canon and offer some fine historical mystery writing.

Thou Shalt Not Kill. Anne Perry, ed. 2005. Carroll and Graf, ISBN 0786715758, 284p.

The Bible is filled with smiting and death, especially the Old Testament. The stories here all offer takes on incidents from the Bible, and they range from the humorous to the unsettling. The tales come from the pens of acclaimed crime novelists such as Simon Brett, Carole Nelson Douglas, Peter Robinson, Anne Perry, and Sharan Newman.

"Words Are Loaded Pistols" (Jean-Paul Sartre): Philosophical Mysteries

It is not uncommon for writers to use crime fiction to explore ideas about society and the world around us. These authors use the themes of the crime novel, good versus evil, crime and punishment, truth and falsehood, as jumping-off points for their philosophical excursions. Their stories often open our eyes to new ways of looking at the world, even as we enjoy the thrills and puzzles of a mystery novel. On this list you will find a variety of philosophies explored, from Native American to medieval to Zen. So think, if a gun is fired but no one hears it, did someone get shot?

Anaya, Rudolpho
Zia Summer. **Sonny Baca mysteries.** 1996. Warner Books, ISBN 0446603163, 368p.

Anaya writes his mysteries with a strong sense of the spiritual and philosophical traditions of the Chicano and Native American cultures of the U.S. Southwest. An element of mysticism pervades the story as Albuquerque private investigator Sonny Baca investigates the gruesome murder of his cousin.

Eco, Umberto
➩ *The Name of the Rose*. 2006. Everyman's Library, ISBN 0307264890, 600p.

Aristotle's lost second book of the Poetics, dealing with comedy, is at the heart of this philosophical thriller. Set in the 1320s, Franciscan Brother William Baskerville is sent to investigate heresy charges in an Italian monastery. The conflict here is between reason and faith. Eco, a semiotician, has created a rich portrayal of medieval thought as well as a compelling mystery.

James, P. D.
A Taste for Death. **Adam Dalgliesh mysteries.** 1998. Ballantine, ISBN 0345430581, 480p.

James's Adam Dalgliesh series often explores the consequences of actions taken or not taken. Dalgliesh is one of the most introspective of English detectives, a poet as well as a Scotland Yard inspector. Here, Dalgliesh and his team are called in to investigate a double killing involving a respected politician and an indigent. Dalgliesh slowly peels away facades to get at the core of truth about the deaths.

Lehane, Dennis
Mystic River. 2002. HarperTorch, ISBN 0380731851, 496p.

The examined life is a centerpiece of philosophy and also the center of Lehane's bleak and somber tale. Three men's lives are tied together by experiences of their youth and a present-day crime. Lehane relentlessly depicts how the past influences the present as the three former friends react to the killing of one of the men's daughter.

Malone, Michael
Time's Witness. **Hillston mysteries.** 2002. Sourcebooks, ISBN 1570717540, 576p.

Malone's novel explores the idea of revenge and the impact of the death penalty on criminal and victim alike in this tense and thoughtful story. Set in the North Carolina Piedmont and narrated by local boy and Chief of Police Cuddy Mangum, the novel focuses on the gray areas in which right and wrong are less than clearly defined. Mangum and his lieutenant investigate the killing of a black activist, whose brother is on death row.

McCall Smith, Alexander
The Sunday Philosophy Club. **Isabel Dalhousie mysteries.** 2004. Pantheon, ISBN 0375422986, 256p.

Isabel Dalhousie, editor of *Review of Applied Ethics,* is the appealing sleuth in the first of McCall's Sunday Philosophy Club series. The club meets under Dalhousie's leadership (though there is not a meeting in this book). Dalhousie's philosophical approach takes on a more practical test when she feels compelled to investigate the death of a young man who fell from a theater balcony after a concert.

Pears, Iain

An Instance of the Fingerpost. 1999. Berkley, ISBN 0425167720, 752p.

> Pears's layered mystery, set in seventeenth-century England, looks at the murder of Oxford professor Robert Grove through the eyes of four different narrators. Each narrator places the events of the death in the frame of his own philosophical leanings. In the end, it is hard to say which of them has the truth of the matter. Pears tells a complex story that examines the conflict between faith and reason.

Van de Wetering, Janwillem

The Rattle-Rat. **Grijpstra and de Gier mysteries.** 1997. Soho Crime, ISBN 1569471037, 294p.

> Van de Wetering is a scholar of Zen Buddhism, and his series featuring the Amsterdam, Netherlands, murder squad is as complex as any Zen koan. The writing is spare and elegant, tuned to the rhythms of jazz music and Buddhist concepts of cessation of desire and right action. Here, a local killing takes the squad to rural Friesland, where they find a complex series of links that finally lead them to the killer.

Murder, I Wrote: Crime Stories in the First Person

Much crime fiction is told in the third person, with the narrator taking a broad view of the situation and describing the actions and motivations of investigator and criminal alike. But some of the most interesting mystery stories are told by the detective, and the reader knows only as much as the investigator does and can make deductions and conclusions along with the detective. Much of the appeal here is in the character of the narrator and the skill with which they tell the story. Here are some excellent examples of first-person crime stories.

Adams, Harold

Lead So I Can Follow. **Carl Wilcox mysteries.** 2000. Walker, ISBN 0802775969, 224p.

> Written in clear and straightforward prose, Adams's stories follow the trail of wandering sign painter and sometime detective Carl Wilcox during the Great Depression. Wilcox is a superb narrator, and Adams captures the feel of rural life in the Midwest during the 1930s. Here, Wilcox and his new bride find the calm of their canoe trip honeymoon broken when a young musician falls to his death from a cliff near their campsite. Their investigation into the death turns complex in what *Booklist* called the "best series many mystery fans have never read."

Burke, Alafair
Judgment Calls. **Samantha Kincaid mysteries.** 2004. St. Martin's Paperbacks, ISBN 0312997205, 368p.

Burke's quick moving, tightly plotted series starter introduces Multnomah County (Washington) Deputy District Attorney Samantha Kincaid. Kincaid is an appealing narrator, and Burke has a feel for dialogue (perhaps it's genetic; her father is noted crime novelist James Lee Burke). Kincaid gets her first big case when a young runaway is left for dead in the Columbia River gorge. Kincaid's investigation turns up a teen prostitution ring, and the dangers multiply.

Burke, James Lee
⇨ *Heaven's Prisoners.* **Dave Robicheaux mysteries.** 2002. Pocket, ISBN 0743449193, 320p.

There are few writers of crime fiction as adept at character and dialogue as Burke. Robicheaux is a complex character who makes a wonderful narrator. He is prone to violence and alcohol but constantly struggling to live up to his moral code. When he and his wife see a plane go down in the Gulf of Mexico, they rescue the only survivor, a young Latina. But their act of mercy puts all three in danger and brings deep sorrow to Robicheaux's life.

Davis, Lindsey
A Body in the Bath House. **Marcus Didius Falco mysteries.** 2003. Mysterious Press, ISBN 0446691704, 368p.

The first-person mystery offers plenty of opportunities for humor, especially if your narrator is wisecracking and cynical PI Marcus Didius Falco. Set in first-century Rome, the Falco mysteries endear themselves to the reader with their mix of hard-boiled narrative and historical detail. Here, Falco ends up traveling to the ends of the Empire, Magna Britannia, to settle problems at a major building site.

Grabenstein, Chris
Tilt a Whirl. **Jersey Shore mysteries.** 2006. Carroll and Graf, ISBN 0786717815, 321p.

Grabenstein's series debut introduces us to two appealing characters, ex-army MP John Ceepak, now working as a cop in Sea Haven, New Jersey, and his callow partner, Danny Boyle. The contrast between the dedicated and focused senior cop and narrator Boyle, who signed up as a summer cop to win "young babes," makes for an interesting story. Boyle's appreciation of Ceepak's skills and dedication grows as the pair investigates the death of a local real estate tycoon.

Lopresti, Robert
Such a Killing Crime. 2005. Kearney Street Books, ISBN 0972370633, 262p.

Joe Talley, manager of the folk club The Riding Beggar, is an appealing guide to the 1960s Greenwich Village folk scene. Talley's narration of the story drives the plot, and Lopresti re-creates the sounds and senses of the folk boom. Bob Dylan, Tom Paxton, and Phil Ochs make cameo appearances, and the mystery rings like a well-constructed song.

Schwegel, Theresa
Officer Down. 2006. St. Martin's Paperbacks, ISBN 0312942117, 320p.

The first-person police procedural gives a special insight into the challenging and dangerous life of a law enforcement officer. Chicago PD Officer Samantha Mack finds herself in a tough situation when a bust goes wrong, and she wakes up in the hospital to find that her partner has been killed—with her gun. Mack is an able escort through the sometimes labyrinthine ways of official policing.

Wilson, Laura
A Little Death. 2000. Bantam, ISBN 055358281X, 320p.

It is 1955, and the London police discover the bodies of three elderly people shot to death in an apparent murder-suicide. Their deaths are the culmination of a tragedy that took place long before, and that Wilson explores by offering each of the three as a first-person narrator. Each offers a slightly varied perspective on the earlier tragedy in which they were involved. The three intertwining tales lead to a surprising revelation.

A Most Beautiful Death: Elegantly Written Mysteries

The realm of elegant writing is not limited to the creators of literary fiction. You can find lyrical prose in all of the genres, and the books on the following list are examples of some of the finest writing being done in any form today. If literary snobs ever tell you that crime fiction is second-rate writing, hand them one of these titles and see what they have to say.

Bayard, Louis
Pale Blue Eye. 2007. Harper Perennial, ISBN 0060733985, 448p.

Bayard is known for his lyrical fiction. Here, he skillfully re-creates the West Point of the 1830s as retired detective Gus Landor accepts the school's appeal to investigate a gruesome killing at the academy. Landor enlists the help of a cadet who would come to be known for his own lyrical prose style, Edgar Allan Poe. Bayard creates a beautiful picture using a palate of historical detail and elegant style.

Chandra, Vikram
Sacred Games. 2007. HarperCollins, ISBN 0061130354, 928p.

Chandra's newest book is a sprawling, literary thriller set in Mumbai (formerly Bombay). The story follows the lives of two main characters, Ganesh Gaitonde, a successful Indian gangster, and Sartaj Singh, the Sikh policeman who is pursuing him. But there is much more for the reader in the intricate, densely plotted, and lushly written tale. *Sacred Games* is a richly detailed portrait of Indian life and a fascinating study of good and evil.

Gur, Batya

Murder Duet: A Musical Case. **Michael Ohayon mysteries.** 2000. Harper Paperbacks, ISBN 0060932988, 444p.

The death of Israeli writer Batya Gur in 2005 was a loss to lovers of elegantly written crime fiction. Gur's mysteries featuring Jerusalem Police Superintendent Michael Ohayon blend beautiful descriptions of the Israeli landscape with compelling portraits of characters. In this case, Ohayon investigates the murder of the husband and son of a cellist who is a close friend of Ohayon.

Haddam, Jane

Skeleton Key. **Gregor Demarkian mysteries.** 2001. St. Martin's Minotaur, ISBN 0312978650, 352p.

Haddam's mysteries featuring former FBI agent Gregor Demarkian are noted for their complex plots, multiple characters, and thoughtful writing. In this installment, Demarkian is called in to investigate the murder of a debutante who would have had a substantial inheritance. Haddam captures the feel of small-town life, and the book would be worth reading even if the mystery was not so compelling.

Izzo, Jean-Claude

Chourmo. **Marseilles mysteries.** 2006. Europa Editions, ISBN 1933372176, 243p.

Set in the slums of Marseilles, Izzo's *Chourmo* is a darkly elegant novel in which references to music and poetry blend with a very noirish sensibility. Here, a former Marseilles cop, Fabio Montale, works as a private investigator. When the son of his cousin disappears, Montale's investigation takes him on a violent ride through the dark side of the French port. The mood is somber, but the writing shines through.

James, P. D.

Devices and Desires. **Adam Dalgliesh mysteries.** 2002. Warner Books, ISBN 0446679194, 448p.

James's crime novels can be read as beautifully constructed character studies as much as for the puzzle at the heart of the story. Her plots are dense, and the descriptions of the English countryside make you feel that you are there. Here, Dalgliesh travels to the Norfolk coast to deal with family matters when he is asked to assist in the investigation of a serial killer.

Oleksiw, Susan

Friends and Enemies. **Mellingham mysteries.** 2001. St. Martin's Minotaur, ISBN 0312978650, 352p.

The New England setting is lovingly rendered with care and style in Oleksiw's novels set in small-town Massachusetts. Featuring Police Chief Joe

Silva, the series is noted for its puzzling plots and wide-ranging cast of characters, but the real appeal is Oleksiw's writing. Here, Silva investigates an
assault on a local businessman that is the first of a series of unsettling events
surrounding the 25th reunion of Mellingham High.

Pamuk, Ohan
 ⇨ *My Name Is Red*. 2002. Vintage, ISBN 0375706852, 432p.

My Name Is Red is a lush, complex historical crime novel from the pen of
Turkish writer Pamuk. The story is set in the sixteenth-century court of the sul-
tan, and the deaths of two artists working on a book for the ruler set off a series
of investigations. The story opens with a narration from one of the dead men
and increases in complexity and daring from there. Pamuk presents a fascinating meditation on the role of art in society as well as a plausible mystery.

Index

133

About the Author

 BARRY TROTT is the Director of Adult Services at the Williamsburg (VA) Regional Library. He received his MSLS from The Catholic University of America School of Library and Information Science in 1997, and has worked at the Williamsburg Regional Library as reference librarian and as readers' services librarian prior to becoming division head. Barry is the past-chair of the RUSA CODES Readers' Advisory Committee for ALA, edits the readers' advisory column for *RUSQ*, and writes for the *NoveList* readers' advisory database. In 2007, Barry was awarded both the Public Library Association's Allie Beth Martin Award and the ALA Reference and User Services Association's Margaret E. Monroe Library Adult Services Award in recognition for his work in readers' advisory services.